PRACTICE BOOK

Rare Finds

Harcourt Brace & Company

Orlando Atlanta Austin Boston San Francisco Chicago Dallas New York Toronto London

CONTENTS

Making a Learning Log / 1–2

Guiding Your Way

Mandy Sue Day / 3–9

Justin and the Best Biscuits in the World / 10–16

Mirette on the High Wire / 17–22

Working It Out

Bonesy and Isabel / 23–30

Hugger to the Rescue / 31–37

Felita / 38–46

Teammates / 47–54

Natural Changes

The Great Kapok Tree / 55–60

Jaguarundi / 61–68

Hiding Out / 69–76

Sierra / 77–84

In Search of a Dream

Pioneers / 85–93

Blue Willow / 94–100

The California Gold Rush / 101–109

The Gold Coin / 110–116

Making Progress

The Almond Orchard / 117–123

Extraordinary Black Americans / 124–131

A River Ran Wild / 132–140

Be Kind to Your Mother (Earth) / 141–148

Great Inspirations

The Nightingale / 149–155

A Young Painter / 156–164

Pueblo Storyteller / 165–171

The Skirt / 172–179

Alvin Ailey / 180–187

Skills and Strategies Index / 188–189

Printed in the United States of America

ISBN 0-15-307417-5

10 11 12 13   054   03 02 01

You will need

a notebook or stapled sheets of paper, a pencil, a pen, crayons or markers.

MAKING A LEARNING LOG

Here are some ideas for making and using your Learning Log:

★ Illustrate the cover with drawings that will help make this book a fun place to write.

★ You may want to divide your book into sections. For example, you could keep a section for each subject, or you might divide the book into weeks or months.

★ Keep your Learning Log with you as much as possible. You never know when you'll learn something new.

★ Try to write in your Learning Log at least once each day.

I have sections for Reading, Language, Math, Science, and Social Studies in mine.

I drew a picture of a space shuttle on mine. That reminds me of how much there is to learn.

You can record all kinds of things in your Learning Log:

★ You might **tell *how*** you learned something. ----------→

> *November 11*
> *I learned a great way to summarize. I wrote a one-sentence summary for each section of the article. I highlighted the important words. Then I wrote a new sentence using the highlighted words.*

★ You could **write what you know** and **what you don't know** about a topic. ----------→

> I know that whales are mammals, but I really want to find out whether they have lungs, as most mammals do.

★ You might **write questions** or **list things** you want to learn better. ----------→

> THINGS TO STUDY
> 1. USING <u>LESS</u> OR <u>FEWER</u>
> 2. USING <u>WHO</u> OR <u>WHOM</u>
> 3. USING <u>WHICH</u> OR <u>THAT</u>

★ You can **make diagrams** or **charts**. ----------→

> helps strangers   is kind to animals
>
>   (main character)
>
> works hard   is honest

★ You could **write about** how what you learned could be applied to **other subjects** or your **daily life**. ----------→

> *Using context clues will help me in science. I always seem to run into lots of unfamiliar words in the science textbook.*

Harcourt Brace School Publishers

TRY THIS! Learning Log

Look for the TRY THIS! Learning Log activities throughout this book. They'll give you ideas about other things to write in your Learning Log.

Name _____

Arrange the units of measure from largest to smallest. For each word in the box, decide which list it belongs in. Write it in the best place in the list. (Two of the words are used in the proverb below.)

acres	bale	bushel	day	scoop	second	week

year

_____

month

_____

_____

_____

minute

_____

_____

_____

quart

_____

_____

tablespoon

_____

pinch

_____

An old proverb says:

Give a horse a

_____ of hay, and he will carry you

over many _____.

Think of a word that names a unit of measure. Give a partner clues such as "This is less than a yard but more than an inch." See how long it takes your partner to guess your word. Then switch roles and play again.

Name _____

A. Read each situation. Use what you know about Mandy Sue to predict what she will do next. Then explain your response.

Mandy Sue cannot find a carrot to feed to Ben. She checks around the barn and discovers several small piles of hay.

What will Mandy Sue do?

_____

_____

What makes you think that?

_____

_____

Mandy Sue gets lost while riding in the woods. She smells smoke coming from a neighbor's chimney.

What will Mandy Sue do?

_____

_____

What makes you think that?

_____

_____

During the night, Mandy Sue is awakened by Ben's whinnies and stamping feet. She also hears a cat meowing near Ben's stall.

What will Mandy Sue do?

_____

_____

What makes you think that?

_____

_____

Harcourt Brace School Publishers

Name _____

B. Near the end of the story, Mandy Sue reminds her little brother that she is blind. Until then, it is never mentioned. Yet you may already have guessed it, based on clues you read. Find five sentences in the story that lead you to the conclusion that Mandy Sue is blind. Write them below.

1. _____

_____

2. _____

_____

3. _____

_____

4. _____

_____

5. _____

_____

For a week, try being aware of when you make predictions and draw conclusions. Whenever you go through either process, write down notes about your thinking.

TRY THIS! Learning Log

Justin and the
Best Biscuits
in the World

This poster could be much better. For each group of underlined words, find a word that means the same thing. The words you will need are on the biscuits. Write the word you choose above the underlined words.

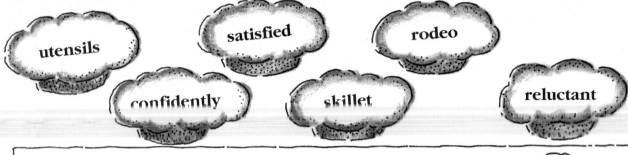

utensils   satisfied   rodeo   confidently   skillet   reluctant

BISCUIT-BAKING CONTEST
3 P.M. SATURDAY

How well do your best biscuits stack up against the competition? Enter this contest and see!

Don't be <u>holding back and unwilling</u> to enter. Just show off

your cooking skills <u>feeling sure of yourself</u>! After all, we're

<u>having no doubts</u> that we have the best bakers in the state!

You won't need to bring your own <u>pots and pans and other cooking tools</u>.

We will have a <u>shallow pan with a handle</u> for each cook to use. Prizes will be

given out Saturday night after the <u>riding and roping</u> contest.
Refreshments will follow—biscuits, of course!

Harcourt Brace School Publishers

TRY THIS!
Writing

Make a word web of cooking words you know. Use at least one of the words on the biscuits.

Name _____

A. Think about the main things that happen in the story. On the left, write what you think will happen. On the right, write what actually happened.

What I Predict Will Happen	What Actually Happened

B. Describe how Justin has changed by the end of the selection.

_____

_____

_____

_____

_____

Name _____

Justin and the
Best Biscuits
in the World

A. Read the sentences in these pictures. Circle each exclamatory sentence, and underline each imperative sentence. Be careful. Some of the sentences are declarative or interrogative.

B. Write your own sentences for the characters in the picture below. Give one character an imperative sentence. Give the other character an exclamatory sentence.

Make your own cartoon. Have your characters say at least three different kinds of sentences. Share your cartoon with a classmate, and explain what makes each sentence the kind it is.

Justin and the
Best Biscuits
in the World

Name _____

A. Justin wrote a rough draft of a letter to his sister Hadiya. Find the twelve misspelled words in his letter. Then write each word correctly.

mean	nest	step	beach	speak	sheet
check	least	else	fence	guess	slept

Dear Hadiya,

    You'll never gess what Grandpa and I have been doing! Yesterday we rode around the ranch to see where the fense needed to be mended. We saw birds and a bird's nes and something els, too—a deer! Grandpa warned me not to stepp on any snakes. He didn't meen to scare me. He just wanted me to be careful.

    We had to chek several miles of fence, and it was a long ride. In some places the ground was rocky, and in others it was as sandy as a beech. When we got home, I was so tired that I could hardly speek. My sheat and pillow looked good! I sleapt for at leest ten hours!

               Love,

               Justin

Corrected Words

1. _____
2. _____
3. _____
4. _____
5. _____
6. _____
7. _____
8. _____
9. _____
10. _____
11. _____
12. _____

B. The words below are missing their double letters. Find the word in the list that fits each group of letters and spaces. Write the word on the line.

13. sme __ __   _____

14. f __ __ d   _____

15. wh __ __ l   _____

16. fr __ __   _____

| feed |
| free |
| smell |
| wheel |

SPELLING: WORDS WITH LONG AND SHORT e

Harcourt Brace School Publishers

Read each word below. First, write its *denotation*, or exact definition. Then write its *connotation*, or what you think of when you hear the word. Tell whether the connotation is positive or negative for you, and explain why.

lush

Denotation: _____

Connotation: _____

Positive or negative? Why? _____

_____

wallowing

Denotation: _____

Connotation: _____

Positive or negative? Why? _____

_____

brand

Denotation: _____

Connotation: _____

Positive or negative? Why? _____

_____

Talking Tip

Choose a classroom object, such as a picture, to describe to a partner. Describe the object using words with a positive connotation. Then challenge your partner to describe the same object using words with a negative connotation.

Justin and the
Best Biscuits
in the World

Name _____

**Read the following advertisement. Then answer
the questions.**

WANTED!

Experienced cowboys for 2,000-head cattle drive from Dallas,
Texas, to Sedalia, Missouri. Three-month trip through dangerous
rattlesnake country. Must own gun. Will be provided with
horses, food, and rope. Must be able to swim.

1. What use do you think the cowboys will have for their guns?

_____

_____

2. What use do you think the cowboys will have for rope?

_____

_____

3. Why do you think swimming is a
   requirement for the cowboys?

   _____

   _____

   _____

Imagine that you are a cowboy on a cattle drive. Predict at least three things
that might happen to you during the trip. Write a description of your
adventures. Then share it with your classmates.

Name _____

Justin and the
Best Biscuits
in the World

Read each paragraph. Put a check mark next to the conclusions you can draw. Then answer the question that follows.

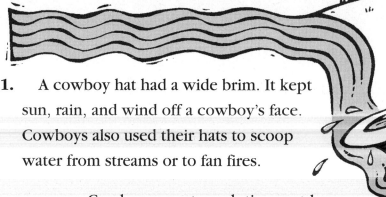

1. A cowboy hat had a wide brim. It kept sun, rain, and wind off a cowboy's face. Cowboys also used their hats to scoop water from streams or to fan fires.

   _____ Cowboys spent much time outdoors.

   _____ A cowboy hat was uncomfortable to wear.

   _____ A cowboy hat was made of strong material.

   What helped you draw your conclusions? _____

   _____

2. American cowboys copied much of the equipment used by Mexican cowboys, called *vaqueros*. The word *buckaroo*, another word for *cowboy*, came from *vaquero*.

   _____ Most American cowboys spoke Spanish.

   _____ Mexican cowboys existed before American cowboys.

   _____ American cowboys bought their equipment in Mexico.

   What helped you draw your conclusion? _____

   _____

Imagine that a visitor comes to your classroom and looks at your desk and books. What conclusions could the person draw about you? Make a list. Then invite a partner to examine your things and draw conclusions. How many conclusions are the same as the ones on your list?

Harcourt Brace School Publishers

Name _____

Cross the high wire by answering the questions correctly. Read each question. On the line with the same number, write a word from the box to answer the question.

enchanted	wavering	boardinghouse
acrobats	agent	protégée	trance

1. Who are performers who do stunts?

2. Which word means "moving back and forth unsteadily"?
3. Who takes care of business for someone else?

1. _____

2. _____

3. _____

4. What is a place to stay that includes a room and meals?
5. Who is a person who learns her work from another person?
6. Which word means "delighted"?
7. What is a word for a dreamlike state?

4. _____

5. _____

6. _____

7. _____

TRY THIS! Writing

Make a poster to advertise a new high-wire act. Use at least one of the words from the box, as well as some colorful drawings. Show your poster to your classmates.

Name _____

**A. Complete the story chart below to
summarize "Mirette on the High Wire."**

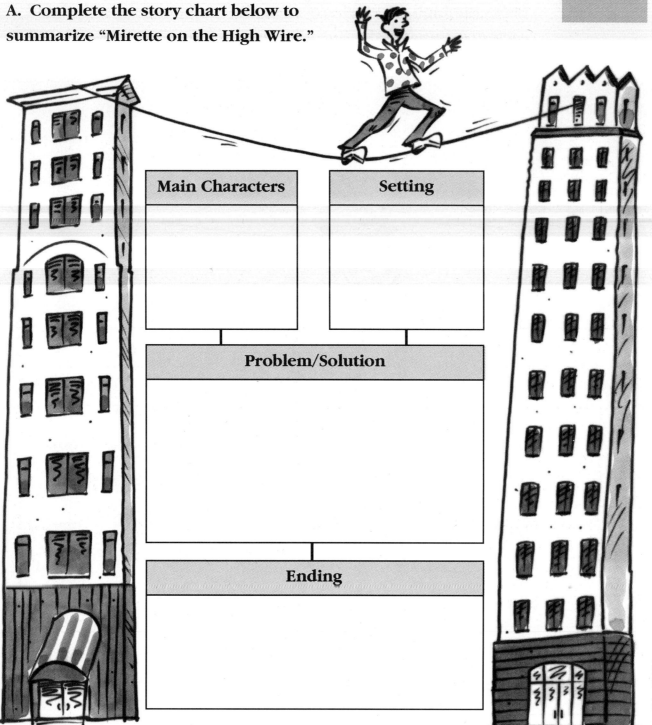

Main Characters

Setting

Problem/Solution

Ending

**B. How does Bellini help Mirette in the story? How does Mirette
help Bellini?**

_____

_____

Name _____

A. The following paragraph is written with simple sentences only. Rewrite the paragraph by combining at least three pairs of simple sentences to make compound sentences.

Eduardo has always loved the circus. Now he is making plans to become a circus performer. He has taken gymnastics classes. His teacher is impressed with Eduardo's skill. Eduardo also belongs to a drama club. He likes performing in all kinds of plays. Comedies are his favorite. Soon Eduardo will have to decide which skills to develop. He may become a circus acrobat. He may decide to become a circus clown.

_____

_____

_____

_____

_____

B. Make up your own sentences about the clowns in the picture.

Write a simple sentence. _____

_____

Write a compound sentence that uses *and*. _____

_____

Write a compound sentence that uses *but*. _____

_____

TRY THIS!
Writing

Write sentences to answer these questions.
- What is the difference between a simple sentence and a compound sentence?
- What are conjunctions? How are they used in compound sentences?

A. Complete the titles of these books about the circus by writing a word from the list on each line. Remember to capitalize the words.

| luck | gold | most | toes | shock | threw | coach | shone |

Walking on My _____
1. Read this exciting story of a ballet dancer who walks on a high wire!

The Spotlight _____ on Me
5. A circus star tells the exciting story of his life.

More Than Good _____
2. A ringmaster tells how to plan an exciting circus career.

Help! The Elephant _____ Me!
6. Laugh along with this funny tale of life as an elephant rider.

How to _____ Acrobats
3. You'll flip over this book! A famous teacher of acrobats tells her secrets.

What a _____ When I Looked Down!
7. A trapeze artist becomes afraid of heights.

Get the _____ out of the Circus
4. This book will add to your enjoyment of circus acts.

Wearing Silver and _____
8. A circus costume maker tells the story behind the fancy costumes.

B. Add or subtract letters from each word below to form one of the words in the list. Write the new word on the line.

| chop | crew | float | flow | jump | stew | stove | stuff |

9. flower – er = _____

13. steam – eam + uff = _____

10. throat – thr + fl = _____

14. stale – ale + ove = _____

11. stop – op + ew = _____

15. cheap – eap + op = _____

12. limp – li + ju = _____

16. crowd – o + e – d = _____

Name _____

A. Read the sentences below. Write *D* beside each direct quotation. Write *I* beside each indirect quotation.

_____ "You have taught me to be brave again," said Bellini.

_____ Mirette smiled. "And you," she said, "have taught me to be joyful!"

_____ Bellini said a world tour would probably be a good idea.

_____ Mirette replied, "Nothing could please me more."

B. Rewrite each indirect quotation below as a direct quotation.

The agent said that the tour would begin in one week.

_____

Mirette asked her mother whether it was all right to travel for two months.

_____

Bellini told his agent that he wanted to return to Niagara Falls.

_____

TRY THIS! Learning Log

Write an example of a direct quotation and an example of an indirect quotation. Label your examples.

Name _____

Read the following passage. Then answer the questions that follow by making predictions or drawing conclusions.

Circus-style acts began thousands of years ago. In ancient Greece, the Olympic Games included men who stood on horses that raced around a track. In ancient Rome, animals were trained to pull wagons. During the Middle Ages, performers on street corners worked with trained bears, horses, and monkeys. Today, modern circus acts include tiger tamers, performing elephants, and bareback horse riders.

1. What do all the circus-style acts above have in common?

_____

2. What would you predict is most dangerous about standing on a horse while it is racing?

_____

_____

3. Which of the circus-style acts above do you conclude is least dangerous? Why?

_____

_____

4. Do you predict that circus acts will remain popular in the future? Why or why not?

_____

_____

TRY THIS! Activity

Take a close look around your classroom. Write down clues you see that hint what your class may be doing later in the day or week. Share your ideas with classmates. See whether they have drawn the same conclusions.

Harcourt Brace School Publishers

Name _____

Gloria is writing a newspaper ad for Adopt–A–Pup Week. Fill in the missing words. The words you will need are on the bones.

companion passersby rambles translation

breeds abandoned

It's ADOPT-A-PUP WEEK
at the Hillcrest Animal Shelter!

Would you like a cocker spaniel, or a beagle, or maybe a German shepherd? We have dogs of all these _____, ready to join your family. Some of them were pets whose families moved away. Others were _____ beside the road, where _____ found them and brought them to us. Any one of them would make a wonderful friend and _____ for a loving owner.

The Hillcrest Animal Shelter is on Beaver Lane, the long dirt road that _____ along the riverbank. We are open every day. Come and visit us during Adopt-a-Pup Week. A wagging tail needs no _____. It means, "I want to be your pet!"

TRY THIS!
Word Play

You can create an acrostic. Choose a vocabulary word and write the letters of it on a sheet of paper, one under the other. Use each letter to begin a word or group of words that tells about a pet.

A. Study these words from the story. Decide whether each word relates to the story's characters, the setting, a problem, or a solution. Write each word in its proper place on the chart.

abandoned	breeds	passersby	rambles	translation

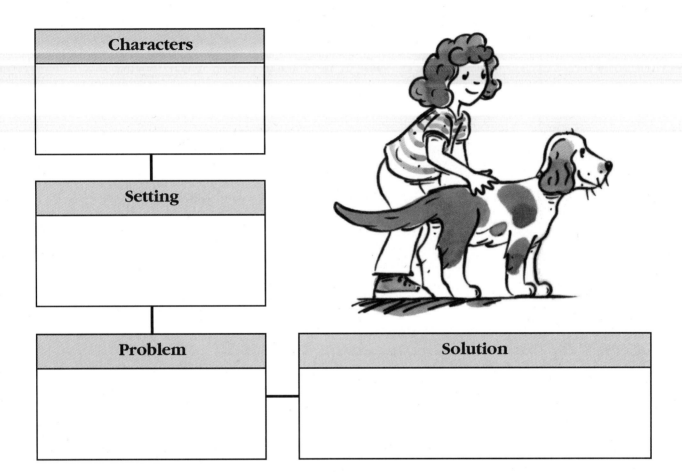

Characters

Setting

Problem

Solution

B. Write a brief summary of the story. Use three Key Words in your sentences.

_____

_____

_____

_____

_____

Name _____

Something's missing. Each word group needs either a subject or a predicate to become a complete sentence. Use each word group to write a sentence of your own. Then write *S* if you added a subject or *P* if you added a predicate.

1. lived together on a small farm

_____

2. a family of ducks

_____

3. dipped their feet into the water

_____

4. made a loud noise during the night

_____

5. a big, strong horse

_____

6. one of the dogs

_____

7. enjoyed visiting the farm

_____

8. the children

_____

Write four words or word groups that could be sentence subjects. Ask a classmate to add predicates to your subjects. Then check to see if each word group is now a complete sentence with a subject and a predicate.

Name _____

A. Have you dreamed of living in the country? The next best thing is to visit. Complete the travel folder by writing a word from the list on each line.

Join us on a _____ through beautiful New England!

It won't be _____ as thrilling as going to the moon, and you won't see any _____ animals. But if you don't _____ a relaxing vacation, our rural New England tour is for you! After seeing the countryside, you can relax by the seashore, but be careful not to burn your _____. For dinner you can order lobster with crab cakes on the _____!

"New England is a favorite vacation spot of _____," says one of our travelers. "The best _____ about it is the wonderful scenery."

Buses will leave on the fourth, _____, and _____ of June. Join us!

side
skin
mine
mind
trip
thing
wild
sixth
fifth
quite

B. Write the word from the list that names each picture.

pie
dishes
gift
type
eyes
lick

_____ _____ _____

_____ _____ _____

RARE FINDS Practice Book

Name _____

Choose the homophone that best completes each sentence, and write it in the blank. Then write a sentence using the word you didn't choose.

hole   whole

1. The _____ farm covered lots of land.

_____

knew   new

2. Isabel _____ almost no English.

_____

rose   rows

3. Emmie arranged her green beans in _____.

_____

died   dyed

4. Everyone was sad that Bonesy had _____.

_____

weight   wait

5. Another stray dog came to _____ for help.

_____

Think of two words that are homophones. Write sentences using the words, but leave a blank space in place of each word. For example, for *through* and *threw*, you could write: *The train went ____ the tunnel. I ____ the ball.* See whether a partner can guess your homophones.

Harcourt Brace School Publishers

A. Read each sentence from the story. Then answer the question that follows.

1. The horses knew the barnyard's circles, the mole and rabbit holes in the fields, the scrambling gravel along the roads, and how far it was from here to most anywhere.
    What does this tell you about the setting of the story?

    _____

2. The animals of Sunbury Road spoke like the wandering mules and chickens and goats from the roads of El Salvador Isabel remembered.
    What does this tell you about the character Isabel?

    _____

3. Whatever language Isabel spoke, Bonesy seemed to know she was saying what his other humans often said: *I care for you.*
    What does this tell you about the character Bonesy?

    _____

4. She held her hand in front of his nose but couldn't feel the little drafts of warm air.
    What does this tell you about the plot of the story?

    _____

5. And in the days that followed, Isabel shared the story of Bonesy's death with each of the animals who lived on Sunbury Road.
    What does this tell you about the story's characters?

    _____

Harcourt Brace School Publishers

Name _____

B. Read the following short story. Then answer the questions that follow.

Sarah sat up straight in the classroom. She listened carefully as the teacher spoke.

"Aloha," the teacher said. "That means 'welcome.' I welcome you to our Hawaiian-language class."

"Aloha," Sarah repeated aloud.

"Are you leaving us already?" the teacher asked. Sarah looked confused.

"I don't understand," Sarah said. "All I said was *aloha,* which means 'welcome.'"

"It does," said the teacher with a smile. "But it also means 'good-bye.'" Everyone laughed, including Sarah.

"That's perfect," she joked, "because my mother says that sometimes I don't know whether I'm coming or going!"

1. Who are the main characters? _____

_____

2. What is the story's setting? _____

_____

3. What problem does Sarah face? _____

_____

4. How is her problem solved? _____

_____

Harcourt Brace School Publishers

TRY THIS!
Learning Log

Describe how you identify the main characters and the setting in a story. Also, tell how you recognize the most important events in the plot.

SCIENCE

A. Read the newspaper article below. Underline each direct quotation. Circle each indirect quotation.

Hooray for Dogs!

NEW YORK CITY—A group of scientists said today that it's time dogs got more respect.

"We're saddened that dogs are treated poorly," said Dr. Kay Nyne, leader of the group. "A dog's life is good, not bad."

The scientists held their conference at the offices of the Dog Society. Society president Dr. Gordon Setter said that dogs are too often taken for granted.

"Consider the ways dogs help us," he said. "They guard homes and stores. They guide the blind. They herd sheep. And they make great companions."

The group's vice president, Dr. Mal A. Mute, said that the English language reflects a negative attitude toward dogs. "People use terms like *dogfight* and *dog days* in negative ways. If something's 'gone to the dogs,' why is that bad?"

Dr. Shep Herder promised that scientists would work to improve the image of dogs in the United States.

"Science has proved the value of dogs," he stated. "They're fetching creatures that are doggone great!"

B. Think of something Dr. Shep Herder might say. Write it here in the form of a direct quotation.

_____

_____

TRY THIS! Writing

Hold a brief conversation with a classmate. Talk about your favorite pets. Then write down what you remember of the conversation. Include direct and indirect quotations. Compare your written version with your classmate's.

Harcourt Brace School Publishers

Name _____

Complete the web by writing the word that fits best on each line. The words you will need are in the dog collars.

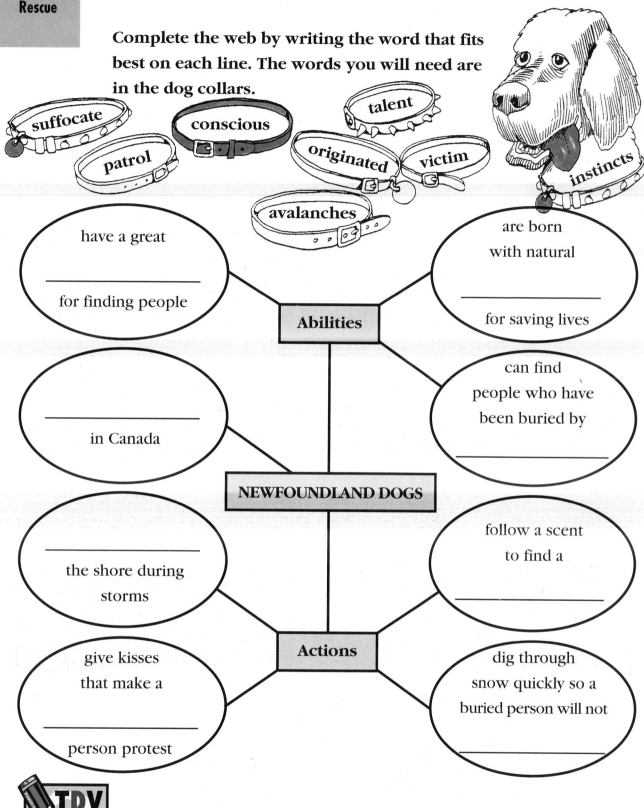

suffocate

patrol

conscious

talent

originated

victim

avalanches

instincts

have a great
_____
for finding people

are born
with natural
_____
for saving lives

Abilities

_____
in Canada

can find
people who have
been buried by
_____

NEWFOUNDLAND DOGS

_____
the shore during
storms

follow a scent
to find a
_____

give kisses
that make a
_____
person protest

Actions

dig through
snow quickly so a
buried person will not
_____

TRY THIS! Writing

Create a newspaper ad that lists the rescue services of Hugger or another Newfoundland dog. Use at least two of the words in the collars.

A. Fill in each column of the K-W-L chart. Use information from the story to fill in the last column.

What I **K**now	What I **W**ant to Know	What I **L**earned

B. Make a list of the reasons Newfoundland dogs make good rescuers.

_____   _____

_____   _____

Harcourt Brace School Publishers

Name _____

A. Read the paragraph, and underline the complete subject in each sentence. Then circle the simple subject. If the sentence has a compound subject, circle both simple subjects.

Dogs and humans have lived together happily for thousands of years. Huge hounds and tiny puppies make great pets. They are good company for their owners. Dogs and their owners enjoy playing and exercising together. Dogs help people in special ways. Specially trained dogs work with police officers. Guide dogs lead blind people. Sled dogs can pull heavy loads through the snow. Most dogs and their owners become best friends!

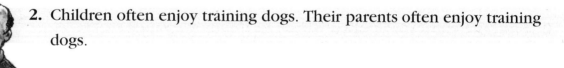

B. Read each set of sentences below. Write one new sentence that has a compound subject.

1. German shepherds can be excellent watchdogs. Doberman pinschers can be excellent watchdogs.

   _____

   _____

2. Children often enjoy training dogs. Their parents often enjoy training dogs.

   _____

   _____

3. Kennels can be good places to find family dogs. Animal shelters can be good places to find family dogs.

   _____

   _____

TRY THIS! **Writing**

Draw pictures of three different animals, or cut three animal pictures from an old magazine. Give your pictures to a partner. Ask your partner to write one sentence about the pictures. All three animals should be named in the compound subject of the sentence.

A. Kona is visiting a fourth-grade class. Finish the students' conversation by filling in the missing words. The words you will need are in the list.

age   city   huge   gentle   pencil   police   voice   college

Kona has a job as a _____ dog!

Kona is more than big! He's _____!

His _____ is five years.

He works in the _____ of Los Angeles.

Kona looks fierce, but he's _____.

He obeys hand and _____ commands.

If I hid this _____, could he find it?

What a smart dog! If he were a human, he'd be in _____!

B. Find the eight misspelled words in this newspaper story. Write the words correctly on the lines below.

bridge   cage   center   edge   judge   once   orange   since

Dog Saves Man from Drowning

A rescue dog named Duke saved a man from drowning today. The man, who was standing on the edj of a brige, slipped and fell into the water. Wonce Duke arrived, wearing his oranje rescue vest, he leaped from his caje. He stopped to juge where the man was. Then he swam into the senter of the rushing river and pulled the man to safety. Sence his daring rescue, Duke has been awarded a silver medal for bravery.

1. _____

2. _____

3. _____

4. _____

5. _____

6. _____

7. _____

8. _____

Name _____

Look at each underlined word. First, write a synonym for the word. Then write an antonym.

Synonym: _____

Antonym: _____

Synonym: _____

Antonym: _____

Synonym: _____

Antonym: _____

Synonym: _____

Antonym: _____

Think of a word. Give several synonyms for the word to a partner. See whether your partner can guess the word. You can play the same game using antonyms instead of synonyms.

A. Write the meaning of each underlined word. Use the word's prefix or suffix for help.

1. A single <u>untrained</u> Newfoundland dog saved a hundred people in one rescue.

   Untrained means _____.

2. Only when she is at work looking for lost people does she <u>willingly</u> leave Susie's side.

   Willingly means _____.

3. Hugger, as his name suggests, is calm and <u>lovable</u>.

   Lovable means _____.

4. The command "Wait" tells the dog to stop and wait for its <u>handler</u> to catch up.

   Handler means _____.

5. If a rescue dog fails to find a victim the first time, it will <u>reexplore</u> the area.

   Reexplore means _____.

6. Newfoundland dogs are eager to learn and quite <u>unafraid</u> of strange areas.

   Unafraid means _____.

7. A Newfie and its handler form a close <u>partnership</u>.

   Partnership means _____.

Harcourt Brace School Publishers

Name _____

B. Help! The search and rescue dogs are looking for words having the same root. In each box below, write three words that have the same root at the left. Then write the meaning of each word at the right. Use a dictionary for extra help.

The root *spec*- means "look" or "see."	

The root *dict*- means "say."	

The root *mot*- means "move."	

motor

spectator
motion

spectacles
spectacular
dictator
dictionary
predict
remote

Knowing a prefix, a suffix, or a root word can help you figure out the meaning of an unfamiliar word. Begin a section of your Learning Log for recording words you come across that have prefixes, suffixes, or Greek or Latin roots. You can use these words in your writing.

TRY THIS!
Learning Log

Harcourt Brace School Publishers

The chart below shows how each vocabulary word is used in "Felita." Complete the chart by telling about a play you have seen or read. Use each word in your own sentence.

Word	Sentence About "Felita"	Your Own Sentence
volunteers	**Volunteers** helped with the sets and costumes.	
audition	Students were asked to **audition** for parts.	
heroine	Priscilla was the **heroine** of the play.	
scenery	Felita made big drawings for the play's **scenery.**	
applause	Gigi enjoyed all the **applause** she got for her good acting.	

TRY THIS! Word Play

Choose one of the vocabulary words, and see how many smaller words you can find hidden in it. For example, you'll find *apple, slap,* and *pulp* in *applause.* Write your words in a list.

Harcourt Brace School Publishers

Name _____

A. Complete the character map below. Include important information about each of the characters.

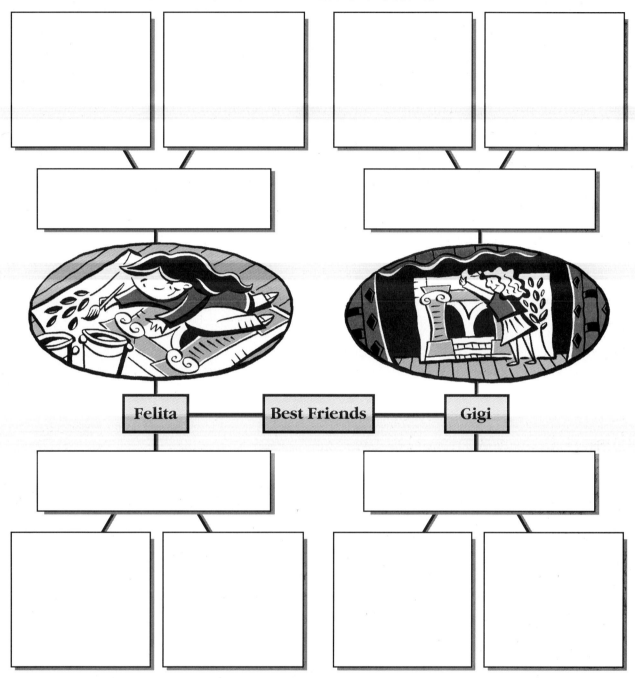

Felita   Best Friends   Gigi

B. Tell what you feel Felita has learned about friendship by the end of the story.

_____

_____

A. Read the paragraph, and underline the complete predicate in each sentence. Then circle the simple predicate. If the sentence has a compound predicate, circle each simple predicate.

Everyone worked hard on the class play. We formed committees and made plans. The script committee discussed the play for hours. The committee members wrote and rewrote the script many times. The final script sounded terrific! The costumes committee worked hard, too. These committee members collected old-fashioned shirts for the cast members. I volunteered for the sets committee. We sketched many different ideas. We chose the best sketch and turned it into a set. We hammered, sawed, and painted for many days.

B. Read each set of sentences below. Write one new sentence that has a compound predicate.

1. The actors read the script. The actors memorized their lines.

_____

2. Our friends arrived early. Our friends found good seats.

_____

3. Everyone in the audience stood up. Everyone in the audience clapped. Everyone in the audience cheered for us.

_____

_____

TRY THIS!
Talking Tip

Tell a partner about a project you have worked on. Use at least one sentence that has a compound predicate. Discuss how using compound predicates makes it easier to tell about a series of steps.

Harcourt Brace School Publishers

Name _____

A. Welcome to the audition! Write a word from the list to complete the description of each part in the school play.

| broom | mood | stupid | wooden | duty | bully |

1. Cindy, a maid who spends her days with her mop and _____

2. Warty, a grouch who is often in a very bad _____

3. Sir Show-Off, a _____ who likes to push people around

4. Juggles, a jester who isn't as _____ as he pretends to be

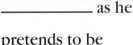

5. Queen Crystal, who never fails to do her _____

6. Timber, a _____ puppet who solves everyone's problems

B. Find the missing consonants. For each word, decide what consonants are needed to form a word from the list. Write the word on the line.

| balloon | fool | goods | into | smooth |
| through | tooth | truth | whom | wool |

7-8. _ o o _ _   _____

or   _____

9. _ a _ _ o o _   _____

10. _ _ _ o u _ _   _____

11. _ _ u _ _   _____

12. _ _ o _   _____

13-14. _ o o _   _____

or   _____

15. _ _ o o _ _   _____

16. i _ _ o   _____

Name _____

A. Many English words come from other languages. Write each word from the ship beside its clue.

1. This word for a special kind of soap comes from Hindi, a language spoken in India.

_____

2. The name for this ring-shaped roll comes from a Yiddish word.

_____

3. This word comes from the Russian word for *astronaut.*

_____

4. This is a musical instrument whose name comes from an Italian word for *soft.*

_____

5. Baked, boiled, or fried, this is a tasty food whose name comes from the Spanish.

_____

B. The names of many American states and cities come from languages other than English. Write each place name beside its meaning.

| Baton Rouge |
| Minnesota |
| Colorado |
| Los Angeles |

1. This state's name comes from the Sioux words for "sky-tinted waters," *minni sota.*

_____

2. This Louisiana city's name comes from the French words for "red stick."

_____

3. This California city received its name from the Spanish words for "the angels."

_____

4. This state should be "colored" red, since its name comes from a Spanish word for "red."

_____

Harcourt Brace School Publishers

Name _____

A. Read each situation. Then write a reason to support each side of the question.

1. Your best friend stars in a play. You think the friend did a poor acting job. Do you tell your friend?

   Yes, because _____.

   No, because _____.

2. You have looked forward to being in the class show, but a play you don't like has been chosen. Do you try out?

   Yes, because _____.

   No, because _____.

3. You and your friend planned to go somewhere, but you learn that a really interesting television special is going to be on. Do you change your plans?

   Yes, because _____.

   No, because _____.

4. Your sister and a friend spend the afternoon at your home. They are telling jokes that you find insulting. Do you say anything?

   Yes, because _____.

   No, because _____.

Harcourt Brace School Publishers

B. Imagine that Felita has written the following letter to a newspaper advice column. How would you answer it? Write your reply below.

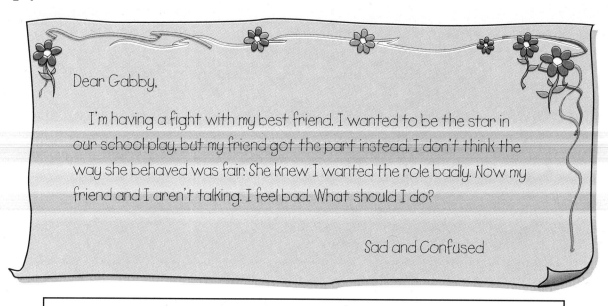

Dear Gabby,

I'm having a fight with my best friend. I wanted to be the star in our school play, but my friend got the part instead. I don't think the way she behaved was fair. She knew I wanted the role badly. Now my friend and I aren't talking. I feel bad. What should I do?

Sad and Confused

Dear Sad and Confused,

Sincerely,

Gabby

Write down the things you think about when making a judgment. Describe the types of information you consider before coming to a decision.

Name _____

Use the chart below to form new words. Choose either a base word or a Greek or Latin root. Then choose a prefix or a suffix. Write the new word you form and its meaning. Then write a sentence for each new word.

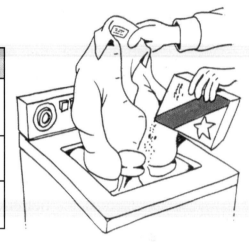

Prefix	Base	Greek/Latin Root	Suffix
un-	taste	*parare* ("get ready")	-ful
re-	kind	*port* ("carry")	-less
pre-	wash		-able

New word and its meaning: _____

_____

New word and its meaning: _____

_____

New word and its meaning: _____

_____

New word and its meaning: _____

_____

With a classmate, read a short newspaper article. See how many words you can find that have a prefix or a suffix. Give yourself one point for every word you identify. Give yourself another point if you can explain the word's meaning.

Read the following lines from a play about the first Thanksgiving. Then answer the questions below.

The First Thanksgiving

PILGRIM #1: Glory be! We've survived nearly a year in our new colony of Massachusetts.

PILGRIM #2: Yes, we are fortunate. Nearly half our fellow settlers died this past winter. Harsh weather!

PILGRIM #1: Indeed, we have much to be thankful for. The corn harvest is thriving. And the Indians have taught us much about the land.

PILGRIM #2: I hear that Governor Bradford has declared a three-day feast.

PILGRIM #1: Yes, it will be quite a celebration! My wife and children are helping to prepare food. My wife is bringing fish, corn bread, and succotash.

PILGRIM #2: The Indians have promised to supply wild turkeys, too. It will truly be a meal of Thanksgiving.

1. What is the setting of the play? _____

_____

2. Who are the characters? _____

_____

3. What problem did the characters face earlier? _____

_____

4. How has the problem been solved? _____

_____

Think of a story from a book, movie, or television show that you know. Make a chart that identifies the setting and main characters. Then identify the plot's problem and solution.

Harcourt Brace School Publishers

Marcus is planning a speech. Fill in the missing words.
The words you will need are on the baseballs.

 hostility

 segregation

 disgraced

 humiliations

 prejudice

Many great baseball players never had the chance to play in the Major Leagues. In the years before laws were passed to end _____, African American players were allowed to play in the Negro Leagues only. Because of racial _____, African American players often could not get rooms in hotels when their teams played in other towns. This was just one of many _____ they faced. When African American players first joined the Major Leagues, they knew their teams would not be _____ by their ball playing. Some fans showed _____ toward these players by yelling angrily. However, things had already begun to change in America. Soon thousands were cheering for Jackie Robinson and other former Negro League players.

Harcourt Brace School Publishers

TRY THIS! Activity

Use a thesaurus or dictionary to find and write a synonym for each of the words on the baseballs. Read each synonym aloud, and ask a classmate to identify the word that matches it.

A. Complete the idea map below.

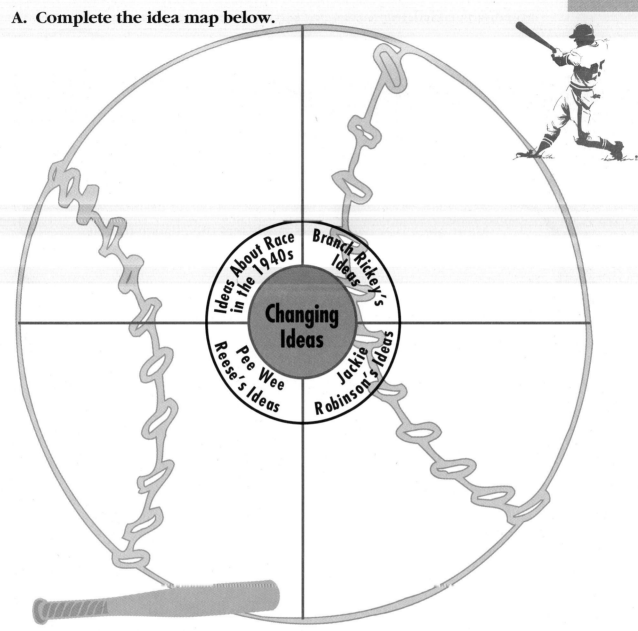

Ideas About Race
in the 1940s

Branch Rickey's
Ideas

**Changing
Ideas**

Pee Wee
Reese's Ideas

Jackie
Robinson's Ideas

**B. Write a brief summary of "Teammates." Use the
information from your idea map to help you.**

_____

_____

_____

_____

_____

Name _____

A. Write a common noun to label the person, place, or thing in each picture.

_____   _____   _____

_____   _____   _____

B. Finish these sentences by writing a proper noun on each line. Follow the clue below the line, and remember to begin each proper noun with a capital letter.

1. Last _____ my favorite baseball team played an important game
   (day of the week)

   against the _____.
   (name of a team)

2. _____ pitched well during the first innings but was replaced by
   (name of a person)

   _____.
   (name of a person)

3. _____ scored the winning run.
   (name of a person)

4. It was a great game, and we all went to _____ to celebrate.
   (name of a place)

Write your answers to these questions.
- What kinds of things would you name by using common nouns? What kinds of things would you name by using proper nouns? Give some examples.
- What do both kinds of nouns have in common?

COMMON AND PROPER NOUNS

A. Complete the signs by writing a word from the list in place of each number. Write the words on the lines below.

dare star parents card morning adore perform rarely

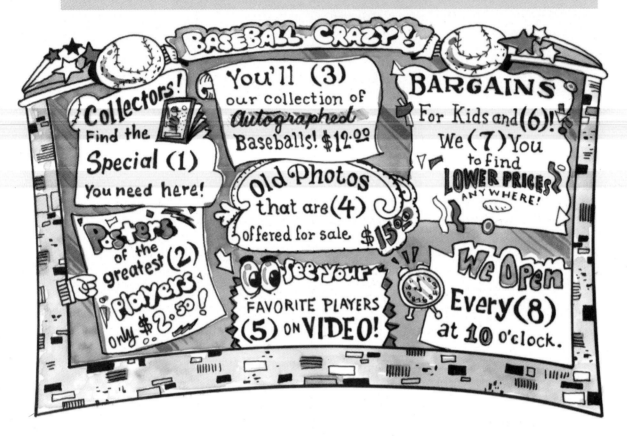

1. _____   5. _____

2. _____   6. _____

3. _____   7. _____

4. _____   8. _____

B. Write a word from the list to complete each group of words.

area court fair garden report stairs therefore yours

9. climb up and down the _____   13. and _____ let me say . . .

10. clay or grass tennis _____   14. write a book _____

11. perimeter and _____ of a rectangle   15. prize pig at the state _____

12. flower _____   16. _____ and mine

Name _____

A. Study the map of Colorado. Then answer the questions.

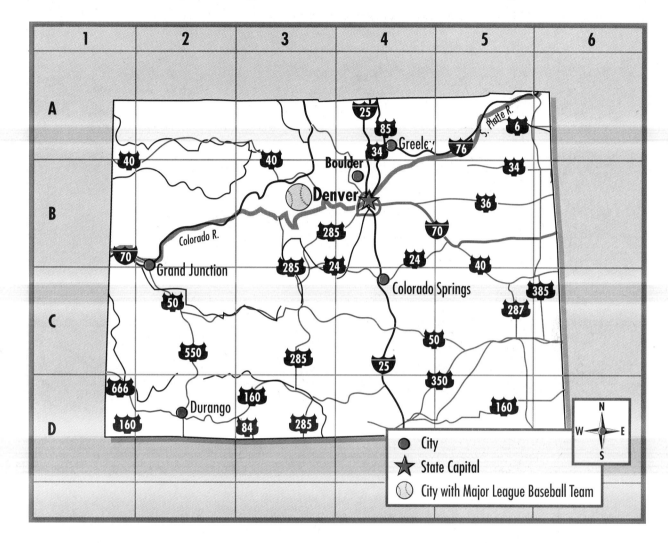

1. Which city on the map has a major league baseball team? _____

2. Which city is located in area B-2? _____

3. Which city is located in area A-4? _____

4. What letter and number tell the location of Boulder on the map?

_____

5. In what direction should a traveler go to get from Colorado Springs to Denver?

_____

6. What is the capital city of Colorado? _____

GO ON

B. Study the graph about the number of people playing youth baseball in the Cedar Hill City League. Then answer the questions.

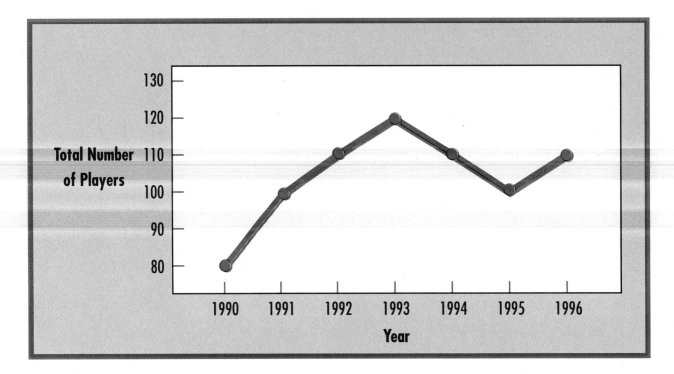

1. What do the numbers across the bottom of the graph tell you?

   _____

2. What do the numbers down the left-hand side tell you?

   _____

3. In which year did the most people play in the league? _____

4. In which year did the fewest play? _____

5. What general statement could you make about the league?

   _____

   _____

Name _____

Read the following story. Then answer the questions that follow.

Jenny was excited when she finally became a member of the baseball team. The all-boy team hadn't wanted her to join, but her cousin Roger had convinced them she would help win games. Roger knew she was a better pitcher than any of the other team members.

Tonight, after six innings, the team was behind 0 to 8. Jenny watched nervously, knowing this might be her chance to pitch. Roger urged the captain to send Jenny in. "What will they think if we send a girl out to pitch?" Jenny heard the captain say. Suddenly she wasn't nervous; she was angry. She walked up and replied, "What will they think if I strike them out?"

"Yeah, give her a try," one boy said. Curiosity was rising. The boys wanted to see what she would do.

When Jenny walked up to the pitcher's mound, there were gasps and then jeers from the other team. When she threw her own special pitch, there was silence. When Jenny struck out the third player, her teammates cheered as she walked back to the dugout.

1. Who is the main character in the story? _____

2. What is the setting of the story? _____

3. What problem does Jenny face? _____

4. What are the main events in the plot? _____

_____

Harcourt Brace School Publishers

Read the following chart. Then use the clues to complete the paragraph.

Prefix	Latin Root	Suffix
un- ("not")	*segregare* ("to separate") *aequalis* ("like")	*-er* ("one who") *-less* ("without") *-ly* ("in the manner of") *-tion* ("the state of")

Branch Rickey wanted to treat the Dodger fans to the best

_____ he could find, _____ of the color of
   (ones who play)   (without regard)

their skin. He thought _____ was _____
                  (state of being separated)   (not fair)

and wanted to give everyone an opportunity to compete

_____ on ballfields across America.
  (in a like manner)

Activity

With a partner, list the base words you find in the answers above. Then see how many new words you can form by giving each base word a different prefix or suffix. For example, you could make the word *replay* from the base word *play*.

Harcourt Brace School Publishers

Name _____

Get to the roots of this tree. Write the answer to each question, using the words on the leaves.

generations

smoldering

emerges

pollen

wondrous

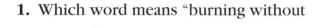

1. Which word means "burning without a flame"? _____

2. What is another word for *marvelous*?

   _____

3. Which word means "comes out"?

   _____

4. What is a powder that fertilizes a flower?

   _____

5. Which is the word for groups of people born at about the same time? _____

TRY THIS! Word Play

Make up your own secret code! Think of a symbol to stand for each letter of the alphabet. Write the vocabulary words, using your symbols in place of the letters. Then trade papers with a classmate. See if you can crack each other's codes.

Name _____

A. Think about the main things that happen in the story. On the left, write what you think will happen. On the right, write what actually happened.

Prediction Chart

What I Predict Will Happen	What Actually Happens

B. What message do you think the author wanted you to get from this story?

_____

_____

_____

Name _____

A. Write a singular noun or a plural noun to label each picture.

_____

_____

_____

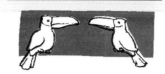

_____

_____

_____

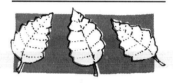

_____

_____

_____

B. Write at least two sentences about this picture. In your sentences, underline each singular noun and circle each plural noun.

_____

_____

_____

_____

TRY THIS! Activity

Many nouns that name animals have unusual plural forms. *Moose* and *mouse* are two examples. Work with a partner. How many animal names with unusual plural forms can you list?

A. Woolly the worm is explaining his feelings to a woodcutter in the rain forest. For each number, write a word from the list. Write the words on the lines.

burn	learn	secure	earth	worker	earn
worm	cure	worse	world	search	worth

Excuse me. Even though I'm only a (1), please don't brush me off. You can (2) a lot from creatures like me. I understand that every (3) needs to (4) a living, but you really shouldn't cut down the rain forest. That's (5) than anything else you could do, except maybe (6) it! The rain forest is (7) more than gold! People all around the (8) need the oxygen its trees produce. Scientists (9) the forest for plants that can be made into medicine to (10) diseases, too. The rain forest is home to so many living creatures! Please leave us a safe, (11) place to live. Now, if you'll just set me down, I'll burrow into the nice, damp (12). Thank you!

1. _____   5. _____   9. _____

2. _____   6. _____   10. _____

3. _____   7. _____   11. _____

4. _____   8. _____   12. _____

B. Write a word from the list that means the opposite of each word below.

curve	fury	curl	pure

13. calm _____

14. polluted _____

15-16. straighten _____

or _____

Name _____

A. Read the paragraph. Then answer the questions that follow.

A year ago Kareem read an article about saving the earth. After thinking about it for a long time, he decided to start an earth club in his neighborhood. He found some others his age who were interested, and they picked a time and place to meet every week. After reading up on local problems, they chose the ones they thought they could best help with. They organized a tree-planting party and then made flyers to put all over town. When dozens of people showed up on tree-planting day, Kareem felt the club was off to a great start.

1. What did Kareem and his friends do before organizing an event?

_____

2. When did they make the flyers? _____

3. How long has Kareem been interested in saving the earth? _____

4. What words and phrases help you follow the order of events in the paragraph?

_____

B. Look at the sequence of pictures. Write a caption for each picture. Use time-order words to help make the order of events clear.

_____

_____

_____

_____

_____

_____

_____

_____

_____

_____

Harcourt Brace School Publishers

TRY THIS! Learning Log

Noticing the sequence of events as you read is important when you study science. Write about ways that understanding the sequence of events might help you follow directions for a science experiment.

Name _____

The nature guide is giving a speech. Fill in the missing words from the list below.

Look over here, and you'll see a _____

tree, which is common to this area. Birds nest in its thorny

branches, and sometimes a red fox _____ nearby,

looking for a mouse for its dinner. This is a kind of tree that can

_____, or fit itself, to the place where it lives.

In this _____ there's plenty of rain, so these

trees grow tall. In the _____, where there is

less rain, they may be only two feet tall. Can you imagine

how you would feel if you were _____ around in

the hot sun, and the tallest tree you could find was two feet tall?

Only a very small animal would be _____ to lie

in the shade of a tree like that!

wandering   habitat   scrubland   content   mesquite   stalks   adapt

Choose one of the vocabulary words, and see how many shorter words you can find by rearranging the letters. For example, you can find *lines* and *nest* hiding in *sentinel*. You may want to challenge a classmate to see who can make a longer list.

A. Complete the story map below.

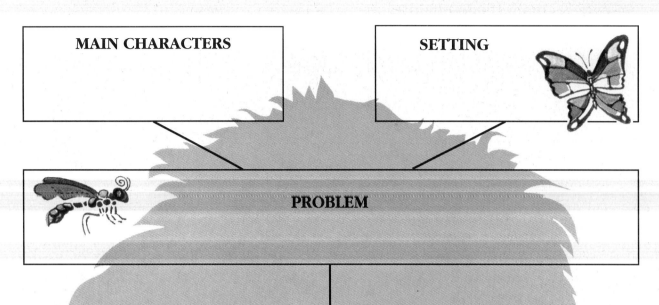

MAIN CHARACTERS	SETTING

PROBLEM

IMPORTANT EVENTS

SOLUTION

B. What message do you think the author wanted you to get from this story?

_____

_____

Name _____

1. the rattles of the sidewinder

2. the perches of the wrens

3. the howls of the coyotes

4. the ears of the rabbits

5. the shade of the cactus

6. the tail of the kangaroo rat

A. Using the possessive form of the noun, rewrite each of the labels on the line with the matching number. The first one has been done for you.

1. _____the sidewinder's rattles_____   4. _____

2. _____   5. _____

3. _____   6. _____

B. Write a sentence about something in the picture. Use the possessive form of a noun in your sentence.

_____

_____

_____

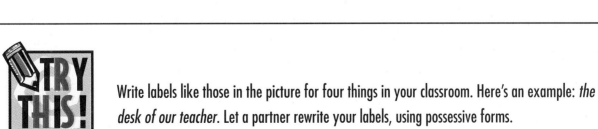

Write labels like those in the picture for four things in your classroom. Here's an example: *the desk of our teacher*. Let a partner rewrite your labels, using possessive forms.

Harcourt Brace School Publishers

A. The king is writing a message. In place of each word or group of words in parentheses, write a word from the list that has the same or almost the same meaning. Write the word you choose on the line.

about	south	around	royal	join	ground
destroy	choice	allow	annoyed	avoid	

Hear ye! Listen and obey this _____ (coming from the king) message! Your king was saddened this morning to learn that there are no longer any squirrels in our land. When we had a large forest, there were squirrels all _____ (nearby), climbing the trees and playing on the _____ (land). They cheered me when I was sad or _____ (upset). Since we made the _____ (result of choosing) to cut down so many trees, the squirrels have gone away to the _____ (opposite of north). Think _____ (of) what we have done! Please _____ (get together) with me in taking action. We must _____ (let) the squirrels to come back, and we must _____ (keep from) having this problem again. We will not _____ (tear down) any more trees!

B. Write the word from the list that names each picture.

crowd
coin
clown
shout
poison

_____ _____ _____

_____ _____

Name _____

Imagine that you have just walked into this picture. What do you see, smell, hear, taste, and feel? Write some descriptive words in the spaces below.

Taste

_____

_____

_____

See

_____

_____

_____

Smell

_____

_____

_____

Hear

_____

_____

_____

Feel

_____

_____

_____

TRY THIS!
Talking Tip

Describe a favorite place to a partner. Use descriptive words to help your partner see, hear, smell, feel, and possibly taste the things around him or her in this place.

A. Read the postcard, looking for causes and effects. Then fill in the information below.

January 16

Dear Kit,

    Coati and I are sorry we had to leave you, but life in our old home was unbearable! Now we have found new homes. We traveled for many days through the scrubland, which made us tired and hungry. We reached the Rio Bravo, but it had too many people, fences, and dogs. So we moved on. I met Red Rundi Cat. The two of us found some shady thickets we like, so we've decided to stay here.

           Your friend,

           Rundi Jaguarundi

Kit Fox
Great Pineapple Field
South of the Rio Bravo

Cause: Life for Coati and Rundi is unbearable.

Effect: _____

Cause: _____
Effect: Coati and Rundi become tired and hungry.

Cause: _____

Cause: _____

Cause: _____
Effect: Coati and Rundi leave the Rio Bravo.

Cause: Rundi and Red Rundi like the thickets.

Effect: _____

Name _____

B. Read the newspaper article below. Then complete the chart to show some causes and effects of moose behavior.

Moose Invade City

ANCHORAGE, Alaska—Several moose wandered into the Anchorage city limits yesterday. They were searching for food.

Moose living in the mountains nearby have been unable to find enough food in the wild because of heavy snow. As a result, they have come into the city, where the weather is warmer and they can find leaves and twigs to eat.

Wandering moose have trampled yards and scattered garbage. During recess time at a local elementary school, a female moose and her two calves strolled onto the playground. Since wild moose can be dangerous, the students had to stay indoors until the family finished a meal of tree leaves and moved on.

Causes of Moose Behavior	Effects of Moose Behavior

Understanding cause and effect is important when you study social studies. Explain how understanding cause and effect can help you when you are reading a newspaper article.

Read the following list of suggestions. Pay attention to the time-order words. Then answer the questions that follow.

Things to Do When Moving
1. Six weeks before moving, notify all magazine and newspaper publishers of your new address.
2. Two weeks later, collect boxes you will need for packing.
3. Next, buy tape and other packing materials.
4. In the final month, begin to pack. First, pack clothing, books, and other items that you do not think you will use during that month.
5. Save for last all items you will need up to the day of the move.
6. Ten days before you move, notify gas, electric, and telephone companies of your departure date.
7. At the same time, notify all friends and relatives, as well as banks and other organizations, of your departure date.

1. What time-order words and phrases help you understand the order of events?

    _____

    _____

2. According to the instructions, how much time is

    suggested for packing? _____

3. Which happens first: notifying friends or

    finishing packing? _____

4. Why do you think the gas, electric, and telephone companies are notified last?

    _____

TRY THIS!

Writing

Think about the most important things you did yesterday. Using time-order words, write a paragraph that describes your day.

Name _____

Share an expert's secrets of survival! Decide which word on the bear's chart answers each clue. Then write the word on the line that has the same number as the clue.

resemble   noticeable   enables
mimic   technique   disguising
surroundings   survival

1. This word means "copy" or "imitate."

   1. _____

2. This word means "a special way of doing something."

   2. _____

3. If you hide the way you look, you're doing this.

   3. _____

4. These are the things around you.

   4. _____

5. This word means "easily seen."

   5. _____

6. This word means "staying alive."

   6. _____

7. This word means "look like."

   7. _____

8. This word means "gives the ability to."

   8. _____

Write three or four of the words from the chart on heavy paper. Cut up the words so that each letter is on a separate square. Mix up the letters, and see how quickly you can put them back in the correct order. For more of a challenge, mix the letters of all the words together! When you get really good, try racing one of your classmates.

A. Complete the Knowledge Chart.

Knowledge Chart

What We Already Know About Animal Camouflage	New Knowledge About Animal Camouflage

B. What is the main idea of the selection you read?

_____

_____

_____

Harcourt Brace School Publishers

Name _____

A. Read the sentences in the pictures. Circle each pronoun.

Are you interested in wild animals, Jed?

Well, Ann, I do sometimes read about them.

Do you know much about leopards? Miss Clark is quite interested in them. She says they can weigh 200 pounds.

Oh, really?

A leopard can jump great distances. It can climb trees, too. Theo thinks that leopards are black, but I don't believe him. Aren't they spotted?

I have no idea. Why are you so interested in leopards?

Maybe you should turn around and see.

B. Write each pronoun you circled. Then, on the same line, write the word or words that each pronoun stands for.

_____   _____

_____   _____

_____   _____

_____   _____

_____   _____

_____   _____

TRY THIS!
Writing

Do you think you would use more pronouns in a paragraph about one character or in a paragraph about lots of characters? Write why you think as you do.

Harcourt Brace School Publishers

Name _____

A. Many animals don't want to be seen! Complete each sentence with a word from the list.

leaving	hiding	stepped	digging
colored	swimming	scared	noticed

I blend in. I'll bet you hardly _____ me.

I have a clever way of _____ myself. I'm _____ green, just like this leaf.

I can hide while I'm _____!

I hide when I am nervous or _____.

I'm _____ into the sand so I'll be hard to see.

Hey! You almost _____ on me!

I don't see any animals, so I'm _____ this place! Good-bye!

B. Write the word from the list that each rebus puzzle stands for.

spotted	printed	tired	driving
skating	chewing	beginning	hated

1.  + d = _____

2. s + (pot) + ed = _____

3. chew + (wing) = _____

4. pr + (IN) + ted = _____

5. (tire) + ted = _____

6. s + (Kate) + ing = _____

7. (Begin +) + ning = _____

8. (drive) + ving = _____

RARE FINDS Practice Book

Name _____

A. Read each paragraph. Write whether the paragraph is organized according to sequence or main idea and details.

1.   Turtles and armadillos both have hard shells for protection against enemies. Turtles go into their shell until danger has passed. Armadillos simply roll up tightly into a ball.

_____

2.   The female sea turtle first digs a hole on the beach. Then she lays her eggs in the sand. Next, she covers them with sand, and finally she returns to the sea.

_____

3.   The toucan is a large, colorful bird. Its enormous bill may be black, brown, green, red, white, or yellow. Toucans grow to be 13 to 25 inches long. Their narrow tongue looks somewhat like a feather.

_____

4.   All the animals except one used speed to avoid the approaching tiger. First, the gazelles, which can travel 50 miles per hour, began to run. Then the zebras panicked and charged behind them. Finally, the tiger approached the remaining animal in the grass—a rabbit. The tiny creature looked directly at the tiger and then scooted into a hole and out of danger.

_____

GO ON

B. Choose your favorite animal. Share information about the animal by writing a paragraph about it. Write one paragraph stating a main idea and details. Write another paragraph using time order, or sequence.

Topic: _____

Type of Organization: _____

Information: _____

_____

_____

_____

_____

Type of Organization: _____

Information: _____

_____

_____

_____

_____

Describe two basic ways to organize information in expository text. Explain how recognizing the method of organization in an article or a paragraph can help you understand it.

Name _____

SCIENCE

Read each situation below. Write a possible cause for what is happening. Then write two possible effects of what is happening.

1. A fox sneaks up on a henhouse.

Possible cause: _____

Possible effect: _____

Possible effect
of first effect: _____

2. An opossum pretends to be dead.

Possible cause: _____

Possible effect: _____

Possible effect
of first effect: _____

3. A chameleon changes color.

Possible cause: _____

Possible effect: _____

Possible effect
of first effect: _____

TRY THIS! Activity

Go outdoors and watch something happening. Describe what you see.
Then write one cause and one effect of the event.

Harcourt Brace School Publishers

Name _____

SCIENCE Read the following paragraph from a science article. Then answer the questions below.

The life of a butterfly begins when a female butterfly lays her eggs. After some time, a caterpillar emerges from each egg. At first, it is a thin creature, but it eats and eats, shedding its skin several times as it grows. Next, the caterpillar climbs onto a leaf or twig and makes a chrysalis. It hangs inside this chrysalis. Later, this outer covering splits in half. Finally, when it opens, a butterfly emerges.

1. What happens first after a butterfly lays her eggs?

_____

2. What happens before the caterpillar climbs on a leaf or twig to make a chrysalis?

_____

3. What is the final step in the process?

_____

4. What time-order words do you find in the article?

_____

Create a schedule that lists the main things you did or plan to do today, hour by hour. Then, on another sheet of paper, write the list in the wrong order. See how close a classmate can come to listing all the events in order.

Harcourt Brace School Publishers

Name _____

Read each word and its definition. Then fill in the missing words in the story Grandmother is telling.

Word	Definition
sentinel	guard or watcher
rodents	sharp-toothed mammals, such as mice
era	period of time
sculpted	carved, shaped, or molded
mantle	anything that covers or hides
reside	live in a place

When I was a girl, I used to _____ in the

mountains. The peaks had been formed in a long-ago

_____, and over thousands of years they had been

_____ by glaciers into rough shapes. One very tall

peak stood like a _____ looking out over the land.

Many kinds of animals lived there, from huge elk to tiny

_____. The mountains were most beautiful to me

when they were covered with a _____ of snow.

TRY THIS! Writing

Choose a vocabulary word, and list other words that it makes you think of. Use some of the words you've listed to write a poem about a mountain, a desert, or something else in nature.

VOCABULARY 77

A. Mark each statement in the Anticipation Guide as T for *true* or F for *false*. If a statement is false, rewrite it on the lines below so that it becomes true.

Anticipation Guide

_____ **1.** The Sierra Nevada mountain range was formed by volcanoes.

_____ **2.** A tree cannot live for thousands of years.

_____ **3.** Predators, or meat eaters, are important in nature.

_____ **4.** A mountain can disappear over time.

_____

_____

_____

B. Write a brief summary of the selection.

_____

_____

_____

_____

Harcourt Brace School Publishers

Name _____

A. Complete the sentences in the picture. Write a possessive pronoun on each line.

Let's stop. These boots are hurting _____ feet.

_____ boots can't be as tight as _____ !

Glenn and Gary both have _____ backpacks, and Sally has _____. Maybe Max left _____ beside the trail.

Look, here comes Max. I wonder where _____ backpack is.

Did you hear that Miss Chen saw a snake? I hope it stays in _____ hole while we go back down!

Those little birds are flying out of _____ nest.

B. Write your own sentence about the picture. Use at least one possessive pronoun.

_____

_____

TRY THIS!
Talking Tip

Tell a partner about a trip you have been on or a trip you would like to take. Use at least two possessive pronouns.

**A. Chad sent a postcard from California to his neighbors.
Write a word from the list on each line.**

Dear Mr. and Mrs. Jackson,

Today we saw a forest of redwood trees that are more than 200 feet in _____! They look as if they could _____ a hole in the clouds! On some older trees, the lowest branches are seventy or _____ feet from the ground. It gave me a _____ feeling to stand under such huge trees. It's hard to _____, but _____ seeds are so tiny that 123,000 of them _____ only a pound.

My parents say they aren't ready for our vacation to be over. I'm not _____, but we'll be coming home Friday. Tell all our other _____ "Hello" for me!

Your _____,
Chad

either	their
friend	pierce
height	eighty
believe	weigh
neighbors	weird

B. Write the word from the list that fits each category.

chief   eighteen   field   neither   thief   weight

Number

Place to Play

Criminal

1. _____   2. _____   3. _____

Negative

Kind of Measure

Leader

4. _____   5. _____   6. _____

Name _____

Draw a picture to complete each analogy. Then write a word that identifies each picture in the analogy.

 is to  as  is to

_____ _____ _____ _____

 is to  as  is to

_____ _____ _____ _____

 is to  as  is to

_____ _____ _____ _____

 is to  as  is to

_____ _____ _____ _____

Harcourt Brace School Publishers

With a partner, write the names of different things on separate index cards. Take turns picking a card. See if you and your partner can create an analogy using the word on the card. Then pick another card and play again!

A. Read each example of figurative language. In your own words, tell what it means.

1. The mountain stands like a sentinel.

   Meaning: _____

2. Meadows nestle in between the arms of forests.

   Meaning: _____

3. The swaying branches sing in gentle breezes.

   Meaning: _____

4. The sequoias have watched three thousand years go by.

   Meaning: _____

5. The mountain cannot hide in the path of clouds that embrace its shoulders.

   Meaning: _____

6. Mountains live and mountains die.

   Meaning: _____

Harcourt Brace School Publishers

Name _____

B. Rewrite each statement below. State the same idea, but use a simile, a metaphor, or personification.

1. A heavy rainstorm fell on the mountain.

_____

2. Daffodils blew in the breeze.

_____

3. A bolt of lightning struck the tree.

_____

4. The round, white moon shone brightly overhead.

_____

5. A wolf howled in the forest.

_____

How does figurative language make descriptive writing more interesting to read?
Write your answer.

Wind and rain are both causes of the mountain's being worn away. Write some other effects for each of these causes.

Wind	Rain
_____	_____
_____	_____
_____	_____
_____	_____

Sometimes several causes can work together to produce one overall effect. See how many causes you can think of to add to this diagram.

Ways Humans Harm the Mountain

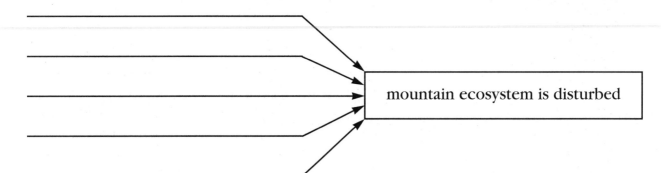

mountain ecosystem is disturbed

Harcourt Brace School Publishers

TRY THIS! Activity

Write both a cause and an effect of a particular event. Share them, and see whether a classmate can guess what the event is. Then try to guess your classmate's event.

Name _____

John and Sally are pioneers who want to tell you about their new home. Fill in the missing words from the list in the box.

opportunities	cautiously	settlers	determination
frontier	succeed	supply	

Hello! We are _____ here in the West. We left

our home back East and came to the _____

because Father wanted his own land. He says there are many

_____ here for hardworking people. While

we are clearing the land and waiting for our crops to grow, the

forest and stream will _____ us with food. Living

here isn't always easy, but our family has the strength and

_____ to build a farm. We're sure we will

_____ at growing fine crops. But right now the

land is still wild, so we walk _____. There are

bears in the forest!

TRY THIS!
Word Play

See how many smaller words you can find already spelled out in the words in the box. For example, there's *tie* in *frontier*. Compare lists with a classmate to see who has found more words.

A. Complete the time line. Write the main accomplishments of pioneers who settled in the West in the 1800s.

early 1800s	1840s	1850s	1890s

B. Describe the main ways pioneers changed the United States in the 1800s.

_____

_____

_____

_____

_____

Name _____

A. Read the following paragraph. Underline each adjective. Draw a second line under each article.

The families checked the wagons carefully. Were the harnesses ready? Two strong oxen would pull each wagon, and many families were bringing several extra oxen. Tomorrow would be the first day of the long journey on the Oregon Trail. In six months, each family would be in a new home in the West.

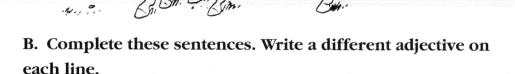

B. Complete these sentences. Write a different adjective on each line.

1. The children felt _____ about the _____ trip.

2. They expected to see _____ animals, _____ trees, and _____ flowers.

3. Their parents worried about traveling over _____ mountains and through _____, _____ deserts.

4. Families felt _____ about leaving their _____ friends behind.

5. Still, they hoped that the _____ trip would be a(n) _____ adventure.

TRY THIS! Writing

If you were moving and could only take a few special belongings, you would want to make sure the right ones got packed. How could using adjectives help you describe things to a mover? Write a list of things you want packed. Describe your belongings carefully.

ADJECTIVES AND ARTICLES **87**

Name _____

A. Use words from the list to complete the newspaper stories.

| cowboy | afternoon | newspaper | good-bye | themselves |
| nothing | nobody | somehow | vice president | |

SILVER CREEK NEWS

All the News from Silver Creek, Colorado   Vol. 4, No. 15   May 23, 1872

MINER FINDS NEW SILVER MINE

Jacob Fielding, prospecting in the hills north of town late yesterday

_____, discovered a load of silver ready and waiting to be mined.

"It's pretty deep in the ground," said Fielding, "but I'll get it out _____."

Fielding has already filed a claim to the new mine. "That silver is mine, and

_____ else can have it," he said. "People who want silver should

go out and find it for _____."

BANK REPORTS LOSS

J.C.R. Smith, _____ of the Silver Creek Bank, reports that

almost $5,000 in gold disappeared from the bank last week. "I first noticed it missing

right after that new _____ rode into town. I looked into the safe,

and _____ was there," said Mr. Smith.

Please contact us at the Silver Creek _____ office if you know

anything about the missing gold.

SCHOOL PRESENTS PROGRAM

Everybody is invited to the program at the school tonight at eight o'clock. Miss

Rose is leaving at the end of this term, so come and say _____.

B. Take a hint! Write the word from the list that fits each clue.

| drive-in | ice cream | life jacket | home run |
| middle school | sleeping bag | snowstorm | |

1. Order from your car at a _____.

2. Hit a _____.

3. It's a blizzard! _____

4. Wear this in a boat. _____

5. You go there after elementary school.

_____

6. Sleep in one outside. _____

7. Eat this on a hot day. _____

Harcourt Brace School Publishers

Name _____

Write a synonym for the underlined word in each sentence.

1. Pioneers had to be very brave.

   Synonym: _____

2. Pioneers faced hardships.

   Synonym: _____

3. Thanks to their help, many new cities grew.

   Synonym: _____

4. The mountain men played an essential role.

   Synonym: _____

5. Mountain men relied on their horses and guns.

   Synonym: _____

6. Native Americans often assisted the mountain men.

   Synonym: _____

7. Stories of the pioneers live on today.

   Synonym: _____

8. They succeeded in finding great opportunities.

   Synonym: _____

Choose a word that names an action. See how many synonyms for that word you and a partner can list in a short time. Then choose another word and play again.

Harcourt Brace School Publishers

SYNONYMS 89

A. Imagine that you are a newspaper writer in the 1800s. Make a list of details you would include in each article below.

PIONEERS SEEK TO FULFILL DREAMS!

_____

_____

_____

_____

MOUNTAIN MEN BUSY IN WEST!

_____

_____

_____

_____

PIONEERS CLEAR FORESTS!

_____

_____

_____

_____

Harcourt Brace School Publishers

Name _____

B. Imagine that you are a Western pioneer in the 1800s. Read the main idea in each letter below. Write details that tell more about the main idea.

Dear Uncle Jed,

The frontier is a dangerous place! _____

_____

_____

_____

Dear Cousin Rachel,

I've never worked so hard in my life! _____

_____

_____

_____

Understanding main ideas and details is important when you share information with others. Write how knowing main ideas and details can help you in giving a social studies report to classmates.

Harcourt Brace School Publishers

**A. Read each paragraph. Decide
whether the type of organization
is *main idea and details* or *sequence*.
Then explain how you can tell.**

1.   The astronauts of the twentieth century are like the pioneers of the
nineteenth century. Like the pioneers, they bravely explore new
territories. Also, they are willing to face danger and hardships.

The type of organization is _____.

I know this because _____

_____.

2.   The space program has several goals. One is to gain a better
understanding of the solar system. Another is to establish satellites to
improve worldwide communication. A third goal is to explore the
possibility of living in outer space.

The type of organization is _____.

I know this because _____

_____.

3.   The space age began in 1957 when the Soviet Union launched a
satellite to circle the Earth. In 1961 and 1962 the Soviets and the
Americans launched the first crewed missions into space. In 1969 an
American astronaut became the first person ever to walk on the moon.

The type of organization is _____.

I know this because _____

_____.

Name _____

B. **Imagine that you are doing science research.
Read the title of each magazine article you find.
Tell whether you think the organization will be *main
idea and details* or *sequence.***

1. Preparing for a Moon Mission _____

2. Venus and Mars: Major Features

    _____

3. Astronaut's Diary: One Week in Her Life

    _____

4. Why Some People Oppose Future Space Shuttles

    _____

5. Step by Step: The Making of a Spaceship

    _____

6. Day-by-Day Review of *Apollo 13* _____

7. Want to Be an Astronaut?—Skills You Need

    _____

8. NASA's Proud and Happy to Say Why

    _____

TRY THIS! Activity

Scan a newspaper with a classmate. See whether you can find at least one
paragraph that represents each of the different types of organization. Share
the paragraphs with your classmates.

Harcourt Brace School Publishers

Read the story and the questions below. Then write an underlined word from the story to answer each question.

My great-great-grandpa kept a diary about his school days. In those years it was the <u>custom</u> for farm children to attend school only when they weren't needed to help in the fields. Grandpa wrote that the idea of going to school didn't <u>appeal</u> to him at all. He really <u>dreaded</u> starting first grade, but his older sister <u>assured</u> him she would take care of him. Most days they walked to school, but sometimes they rode in their own <u>miniature</u> cart pulled by a little donkey. Grandpa was <u>indifferent</u> to the spelling lessons, but he loved learning to read. I wish I could have seen the <u>expression</u> of joy on his face when he read his first book!

1. If you don't care about something, which word describes the way you feel?

_____

2. What is another word for *tiny*? _____

3. Which word means "looked forward to with fear"? _____

4. Which word means "the look on a person's face that shows his or her feelings"?

_____

5. What is another word for *promised*? _____

6. Which word means "to seem interesting"? _____

7. Which word means "a usual way of doing something"? _____

TRY THIS! Writing

Draw a picture of the first school you went to. Then write a few sentences about your drawing. Use as many of the underlined words from the story as you can.

Name _____

A. One way to summarize a story is to complete a Prediction Chart. Finish the chart below.

Prediction Chart		
Main Characters	**What Will Happen**	**Why It Will Happen**

B. Write a brief summary of the story.

_____

_____

_____

_____

_____

Look at the pictures. Then write sentences about these animals.

tree frog   horned toad   tortoise   lizard

Write a sentence using *smaller.*

_____

_____

Write a sentence using *longer.*

_____

_____

Write a sentence using *bigger.*

_____

_____

Write a sentence using *heaviest.*

_____

_____

Write a sentence using *most interesting.*

_____

_____

TRY THIS!
Talking Tip

With a partner, choose four different animals. Together, discuss those animals. Use adjectives that compare.

Name _____

merry	tiny	plenty	valley	country	deny
journey	hurry	pony	monkey	multiply	
hockey	qualify	chimney	supply	body	

Jodi's grandmother is making a photo album. Finish the caption for each picture by writing words from the list.

This was our school in the deep
_____ at the foot of Trapper
Mountain. It was _____ but big
enough for the few students we had.
There was always smoke rising from the
_____ on cold days. We had to
chop _____ of firewood.

We played _____ on the frozen
pond behind the school. My friends and
I had _____ times skating.

All winter the _____ was covered
with snow, and I had a four-mile
_____ to get to school. I usually
rode my father's _____, Lucky.
Lucky could climb over a snowdrift like
a _____ climbing a tree. He was
never in a _____, but I was! That
trip seemed to freeze every bone in my
_____!

Here I am at age ten, studying my spelling
words. I wanted to _____ for
the county spelling contest. I worked
hard in school to learn to read, spell,
_____, and divide. We didn't have
a very large _____ of books, but
I can't _____ that I got a good
education.

A. Read each passage from the story. Use context clues to figure out the meaning of the word in italics. Write what you think it means. Then use a dictionary to check your answer.

1. Janey was well aware that she could have attended that school, too. There was no law *forbidding* it.

   Forbidding means _____.

2. The camp school would now be a daily and forceful reminder of the fact that she didn't belong, and so she *dreaded* it.

   Dreaded means _____.

3. If only she were being taken to the town school, the one where Lupe and all the other children of the *district* went!

   District means _____.

4. His four tiny feet with their *minute* claws were perfect, and from the fringe of miniature scales outlining what should have been his chin, to the last infinitesimal spike on the end of his brief tail, he was finished and complete.

   Minute means _____.

5. She would *loathe* having anyone refer to her new pet as a horned lizard, and if the new teacher did so, Janey's respect for her as a human being would be completely shattered.

   Loathe means _____.

Harcourt Brace School Publishers

Name _____

**B. Read each word and its meaning.
Then write a sentence using the word.
Add context clues to help other readers
figure out the word's meaning.**

1. The word *loathe* means "to hate."

Your sentence: _____

_____

2. The word *jovial* means "in a very happy mood."

Your sentence: _____

_____

3. The word *obstinate* means "stubborn."

Your sentence: _____

_____

4. The word *assured* means "promised."

Your sentence: _____

_____

Harcourt Brace School Publishers

Explain how using context clues in a sentence may help you understand a word you do not know.

Read each statement. Tell whether you agree or disagree, and why.

1. "Students in this country should attend school on a year-round schedule."

   Your judgment: _____

   _____

2. "Every home should have a personal computer."

   Your judgment: _____

   _____

3. "Taking part in team sports is good for children."

   Your judgment: _____

   _____

4. "Watching television is a bad habit."

   Your judgment: _____

   _____

TRY THIS!
Talking Tip

Find a subject that you and a classmate have different opinions about. Hold a discussion in which you each share your ideas. Be respectful of your classmate's opinion.

Harcourt Brace School Publishers

Name _____

Discover gold, and strike it rich! Read the clue on each miner's tent, and then write the word that fits the clue. The words you will need are on the gold pans.

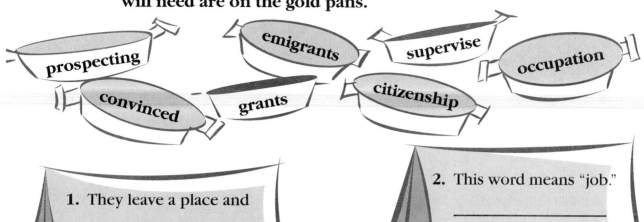

prospecting

emigrants

supervise

occupation

convinced

grants

citizenship

1. They leave a place and settle somewhere else.

_____

2. This word means "job."

_____

3. If you feel sure about something, you are

_____

of it.

4. A person who is looking for gold is doing this.

_____

5. You have this if you are legally a member of a country.

_____

6. These are gifts of land or money.

_____

7. This word means "to direct or manage."

_____.

TRY THIS!
Word Play

Write some riddles about words you know, and give them to a classmate to solve. Use at least one of the words on the pans. Here's an example: What word begins like a tiger's growl and ends with some picnic insects? [Answer: *grants*]

A. Read each statement in the Anticipation Guide. If it is true, write *true*. If a statement is false, rewrite it so that it becomes true.

Anticipation Guide

1. The "forty-niners" got their name because it took forty-nine days to reach California.

   1. _____
   _____
   _____

2. Gold could be found all over the state of California.

   2. _____
   _____
   _____

3. Life in the gold fields was very expensive for the miners.

   3. _____
   _____
   _____

4. Most miners found gold by picking it up off the ground.

   4. _____
   _____
   _____

B. Describe how California changed as a result of the gold rush.

_____
_____
_____

Name _____

**A. Read the following paragraph. Circle the action verb in
each sentence.**

People still search for gold in the Sierra foothills. Families, tourists,
and school groups try the skill of panning. Over and over, they dip
their pans into the stream. They check the pans carefully. Each time,
they hope for a gleam of gold. Most people find only rocks. However,
many return again and again. They enjoy the search!

**B. Complete each sentence by writing an action verb on
the line.**

1. Lettie _____ something in the bottom of the pan.

2. She _____ the small rock carefully.

3. It _____!

4. Lettie _____ to her friends.

5. "Gold! I've found gold!" she _____.

What would you do if you discovered gold? Tell a partner how you would react. Use strong action
verbs in your sentences.

Name _____

A. It's your job to write advertisements for the *Gold Rush Times*! Use words from the list to complete the ads below.

unfair   mistake   disappear
discovery   unhappy   unable
unusual   discomfort

1. DON'T sleep in _____ ! Fanny's Fluffy feather beds will send you off to dreamland!

2. Make dry skin _____ ! use *Lovely Lil's Lotion*!

3. A **SALE** is not complete until you are satisfied. We will have no _____ Customers!

4. AMAZING _____ ! Beauty cream makes ladies look *Their Best*!

5. NO! This is not a _____ Hats are only $20!

6. Were you cheated in an _____ land deal? Attorney Howe I. Fixit can help!

7. VISIT DAISY'S DRESS SHOP for clothing in new styles and colors

8. MINERS!!! Get your gear here. Your money back if you are _____ to find gold!

B. Write the word from the list that means the opposite of each phrase.

dislike   misbehave   misspelled   prehistoric
prepaid   unexpected   unfolds   untie

9. wrote correctly _____

10. like _____

11. wrap a rope around _____

12. just what you thought would happen

_____

13. gave money afterward _____

14. is made known all at once

_____

15. from modern times _____

16. act polite _____

Name _____

Use the clues to identify each English word that comes from Spanish.

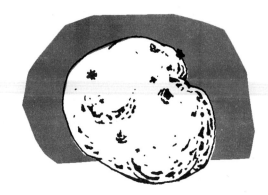

This word comes from the Spanish *lagarto*.

_____

This word comes from the Spanish *patata*.

_____

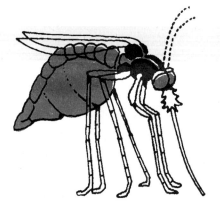

This word comes from the Spanish *corcho*.

_____

This word comes from the Spanish *mosca*.

_____

This word comes from the Spanish *lazo*.

_____

TRY THIS! Game

Play this game with a partner. Using an English-Spanish dictionary, pick out Spanish words that look and sound similar to English words. Write and say each word. See how many English words your partner can guess. Then switch roles and play some more!

Name _____

A. Read each word and its denotation, or exact meaning. Think about the connotation, or suggested meaning, of the word. Then write *positive, negative,* or *neutral* for each word.

Word	Denotation	Connotation
rush	to go with great speed	
location	place	
swarm	large crowd	
precious	valuable	
enterprising	full of energy and daring	
trickle	to flow in a thin stream or drop by drop	
outfit	to equip with clothing or tools	
wealth	riches	

Harcourt Brace School Publishers

Name _____

B. Read the ad. Find three words with a positive connotation and three words with a negative connotation. Write them on the lines.

DON'T SLEEP IN A FILTHY, ICY TENT.

RENT A ROOM AT THE ELEGANT

GOLD RUSH HOTEL

★ SPARKLING CLEAN ROOMS

★ COZY FIRE DOWNSTAIRS

NO SMELLY MINERS ALLOWED.

Positive Connotation	Negative Connotation
1. _____	1. _____
2. _____	2. _____
3. _____	3. _____

C. Imagine the year is 1849. The gold rush has begun, and you have a new ship to take miners to California.

1. What will you name your ship? _____

2. Does the name have a positive or a negative connotation?

_____

Name _____

Use context clues to decide what the words in dark print
would mean if they were real words. Then explain why
your meanings make sense.

1. The 1849 gold rush attracted people from all over
   the country who wanted to become **zablosh**.

   I think **zablosh** must mean _____

   because _____

   _____

   _____.

2. Many sailors left their **blibors** floating in the
   harbor and headed for the California hills.

   I think **blibors** must mean _____

   because _____

   _____

   _____.

3. Working on their knees, miners often wore holes
   in their **drebbies**.

   I think **drebbies** must mean _____

   because _____

   _____

   _____.

Find an article in a recent newspaper or magazine. Underline four words you
do not know. Then see if you and a classmate can find context clues to help you
figure out the word meanings. After making guesses, use a dictionary to check
your answers.

Harcourt Brace School Publishers

Name _____

Read each science report. Write a sentence that states the main idea of the paragraph.

SCIENCE

Some diseases can be spread when people cough or sneeze. Other diseases can be spread by insects such as mosquitoes. Still other diseases are spread by nonliving sources such as the spout of a public drinking fountain.

Main idea: _____

_____

Doctors in the 1850s had few medicines to cure disease. Often they did not even understand the nature of a miner's illness. Today doctors have access to many more medicines and have a far greater understanding of the illnesses they are treating.

Main idea: _____

_____

Coal miners who breathe in coal dust run a risk of developing lung disease. Subway workers exposed to loud noise all day risk a hearing loss. X-ray technicians exposed to radiation run the risk of developing cancer.

Main idea: _____

_____

TRY THIS! Activity

Tell a classmate the ingredients in a particular recipe, such as stew or pudding. See if your classmate can guess the food that is being prepared.

Read each sentence about "The Gold Coin." Then write a complete sentence to answer each question. In your answer, use the underlined word in a way that shows what it means.

1. Searching for the gold drives the thief to despair.
   What might make someone feel despair?

   _____

2. Juan grows impatient when he has to wait.
   When are you impatient?

   _____

3. Juan is stunned, or very surprised, by Doña
   Josefa's actions. What has stunned you?

   _____

4. Doña Josefa helps the recovery of sick people.
   How would you help someone's recovery?

   _____

5. Doña Josefa uses herbs as medicine.
   How might a cook use herbs?

   _____

6. Doña Josefa's ransacked house is a mess.
   What would you do if your desk were ransacked?

   _____

TRY THIS!
Word Play

What's the longest word chain you can create? Start by writing one of the vocabulary words. Circle the last letter of the word, and use that letter to begin a new word. Keep using the last letter as the first letter of a word as long as you can. See how many vocabulary words you can include.

stunn e d e s p a i r

Name _____

A. Complete the character map below. List words and phrases that describe the main characters.

Main Characters

The Thief	The Old Woman

B. Tell how Juan has changed by the end of the story.

_____

_____

_____

_____

_____

Harcourt Brace School Publishers

A. Read the sentences beside each picture. Underline each sentence that has a linking verb. Draw a second line under the linking verb.

Our trip was difficult.
The trail was quite steep.
We all felt tired and hungry.
We wanted a rest.

We ate sandwiches and fruit.
The apples were delicious.
The view was beautiful.
Everyone felt much better.

**B. Write two sentences to go with this picture.
Use linking verbs in both of your sentences.**

_____

_____

_____

_____

Write your answers to these questions.
- How does an action verb help a writer tell what happened? How does a linking verb help?
- What are some examples of linking verbs?

Name _____

A. Carlos has written a fairy tale. In place of each underlined word group, write a word from the list that has the same or almost the same meaning.

pennies
replied
spied
berries
easiest
heavier
hurried
prettier
funniest
multiplied
earlier
memories

THE SPECIAL COIN

Once upon a time, a man was picking small fruits in the woods when he heard singing. He had never heard a more beautiful song. When he looked up, he saw a tiny bird.

"Bird, your song is beautiful," said the man. "It brings back things I remember of past times when I had a pet canary."

"Thank you," answered the bird. "For your kind words, I will give you a coin."

"I am poor and have had few one-cent coins in my life," the man said. "I will hide it."

"Oh, no," said the bird. "That would be the least difficult thing to do, but you must give the coin away. You will find someone who needs it more than you do."

The man thought that was the most humorous thing he had ever heard, but he went quickly away and gave the coin to a boy who had nothing to eat. As the man walked on, he discovered that his pocket seemed more weighty than before. The coin he had given away had increased!

1. _____   5. _____   9. _____

2. _____   6. _____   10. _____

3. _____   7. _____   11. _____

4. _____   8. _____   12. _____

B. Write the word that contains each person's name.

Terri   Art   copies
heaviest
parties
terrified

13. _____   15. _____

Opie   Avi

14. _____   16. _____

Harcourt Brace School Publishers

A. Read each paragraph. Describe the mood or tone that is created. Then identify the specific words or phrases that help create the mood or tone.

It was a dark and stormy night. Tina's car broke down on the muddy, deserted road. In the darkness she heard the screech of an owl. Tina walked to an old house down the road. The porch squeaked as she stepped onto it.

Mood: _____

Words or Phrases: _____

_____

"I feel great!" Grandpa shouted as he leaped from bed. "A great day for fishing in the bright morning sun! And after that, we can go smell the sweet honeysuckle in the park!" Grandpa had a wide grin on his face.

Mood: _____

Words or Phrases: _____

_____

B. Now write your own paragraph. Then describe its mood.

_____

_____

_____

Mood: _____

Words or Phrases: _____

_____

How can you identify the mood or tone of a story you are reading? Explain why it is important to pay attention to details. Also, tell how recognizing the mood helps you enjoy the story.

Harcourt Brace School Publishers

Name _____

A. Read the advertisement. Then answer the questions that follow.

> **Wanted: Hospital volunteers.** Duties include visiting bedridden patients, distributing flowers, bringing supplies to nurses' stations. Must be at least 14 years old. For further information, call 555-3246.

1. What is the main idea of the advertisement?

_____

_____

2. What are the important details given in the ad?

_____

_____

3. What important details do you feel are missing from the ad?

_____

_____

B. Add important details to the following ad:

FOR SALE: Gold coin. _____

_____

_____

Think of something important that has happened to you this week. Make a list of the details and share them with a partner. See if your partner can guess the main idea. Then try to guess your partner's event, based on details given to you.

Name _____

SCIENCE Read each passage. Use the context clues to figure out the meaning of the underlined word. Then use a dictionary to check your answer.

1. Gold is found in <u>lodes</u>. Miners dig in veins in the earth's crust in search of the metal.

   I think *lodes* must mean _____, because

   _____

   _____.

2. Although most gold is taken from underground mines, some gold is also <u>extracted</u> from seawater.

   I think *extracted* must mean _____, because

   _____

   _____.

3. Gold is a <u>malleable</u> metal that can be easily hammered and shaped into any form that is desired.

   I think *malleable* must mean _____, because

   _____

   _____.

Harcourt Brace School Publishers

Find an unfamiliar word in the dictionary. Make up a sentence that uses the word. Include context clues. Share your sentence with a partner. See if he or she can guess the word's meaning!

Name _____

Answer each question, writing one letter of your answer word on each blank. Use each word in the box once. Then unscramble the letters in the almonds to answer the riddle at the bottom of the page.

| yield | mechanical | nourish | cycle |
| quality | silos | nectar |

1. What is the liquid in flowers called?

   ___ ___ ___ ___ ___ ___

2. What are the tall buildings used for storing grain or nuts?

   ___ ___ ___ ___ ___

3. Which word means "operated by a machine"?

   ___ ___ ___ ___ ___ ___ ___ ___ ___ ___

4. What is a word for a set of things that always happen in the same order?

   ___ ___ ___ ___ ___

5. Which word means "keep healthy with food"?

   ___ ___ ___ ___ ___ ___ ___

6. If you check to see how good something is, what are you checking for?

   ___ ___ ___ ___ ___ ___ ___

7. Which word means "the amount produced"? ___ ___ ___ ___ ___

RIDDLE: What does a tree do when it gets bored?

___ ___ ___ ___ ___ V ___ ___!

TRY THIS! Writing

Make up a joke or a riddle like the one on this page. Use at least one of the words in the box. Share your joke or riddle with a classmate.

A. Complete the Venn diagram below by telling what happened in the selection at the beginning and end. Then write the things that happened in the beginning and end that stayed the same.

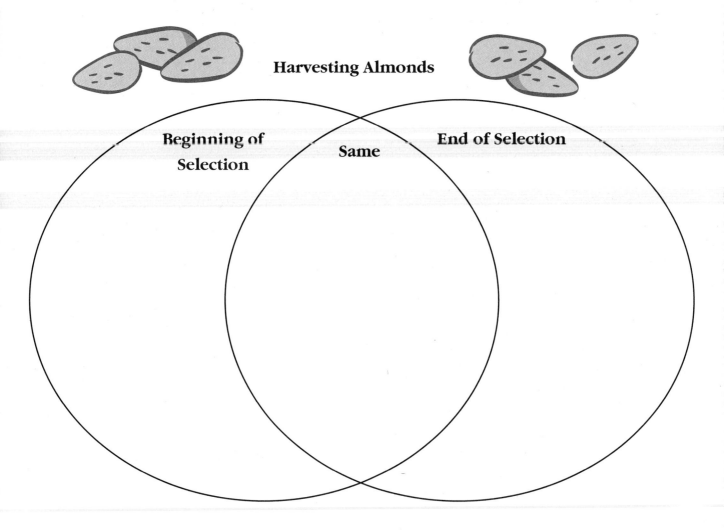

Harvesting Almonds

Beginning of Selection

Same

End of Selection

B. Write a brief summary statement about the selection.

_____

_____

_____

_____

_____

Name _____

A. Underline the verb in each sentence. Then draw a second line under the main verb.

1. People have eaten nuts throughout history.

2. Nuts have provided protein for many people.

3. Nuts will remain fresh in their shells for months.

4. Unusual kinds of nuts are becoming popular snacks.

5. Some food companies are experimenting with new nut products.

B. Complete each sentence by writing a main verb on the line.

6. Jo and Tanya have _____ all the walnuts.

7. They have _____ walnut butter from some of the nuts.

8. Now the friends are _____ open more nuts.

9. They are _____ the nut meats out of the shells.

10. Tanya is _____ some of the nuts.

11. Maybe they will _____ nut bread with these nuts.

TRY THIS!
Writing

Write a sentence about an interesting food you have eaten. Circle the main verbs you use. Next, write a sentence about something you are eating today. Then write one about something you would like to eat in the future. Tell how the verbs are different.

Name _____

A. Find the ten misspelled words in the conversation between the bee and the ant. Write the words correctly on the lines below.

 What a day! I don't rember ever working so hard!

All you did was gathar pollen and necter.

 That's hard laber! You should try working instead of just eating what people leave.

I do work! Today I crawled all the way down to the celler to look for potatoes left in the cornar.

Did you find any?

No, but I got a bite of peanut buttor. Somebody forgot to covor the jar.

Well, climbing jars is easier than flying. These tiny wings have to powar my whole body. I need an electric moter!

corner
power
nectar
motor
butter
cellar
cover
remember
labor
gather

1. _____ 5. _____ 9. _____

2. _____ 6. _____ 10. _____

3. _____ 7. _____

4. _____ 8. _____

B. Write the word from the list that names each picture.

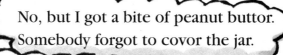

11. _____ 13. _____ 15. _____

12. _____ 14. _____ 16. _____

calendar
doctor
father
finger
letter
paper

Name _____

See how many compound words you can form by joining the names of two pictures below. Then write your own sentences using the compound words you make.

Compound Words: _____

_____

Sentences: _____

_____

_____

TRY THIS! Game

Write five nouns on separate slips of paper. Have a partner do the same. Then mix all the slips and choose any two. Create a compound word from the two words. Make up a definition for it. Form more compound words using the other slips of paper.

A. The letter below was written by the story's narrator to her father. Rewrite the letter in a much shorter form. Summarize the most important information.

Dear Dad,

Last week I visited a factory that makes paper. A supervisor led us around to show us the process. I always thought that all paper was made from wood. But at this factory, it is made from cotton! (That way, no trees have to be cut down.) The cotton is placed in a large vat of water and chemicals. Actually, anything made of cotton can be placed into the vat, like old T-shirts! The material is soaked and mixed until it breaks down and becomes very soft. Then it is poured into a long pan, and a long, flat machine presses on the cotton until all the water is drained out. What's left is a long sheet of paper. When it is dry, it is ready for use—as stationery, for books, or even as printed money!

Love,
Laura

Dear Dad,

_____

_____

_____

_____

_____

_____

_____

Love,

Laura

Name _____

B. Judy and Jimmy have the same ideas, but they say them in different ways. Paraphrase each statement to say the same thing in a different way.

I like the taste of almonds. Sometimes I snack on them after school. Their sweetness makes it hard to stop eating them!

_____
_____
_____
_____
_____

Some almond trees produce bitter almonds. They cannot be eaten. However, the oil from the nuts is used in food flavorings.

_____
_____
_____
_____
_____

Almond trees probably first grew in western Asia. But today they grow mainly in countries bordering the Mediterranean Sea.

_____
_____
_____
_____
_____

TRY THIS!
Learning Log

Explain the steps you follow when summarizing information you have found. Also, why is it important that you paraphrase information in your own words?

Name _____

Read the story below. Use clues in the story to figure out the meaning of each underlined word. Then write each word on the line next to its meaning.

Who ever heard of Oliver Evans? No, he wasn't the <u>orphaned</u> hero of a movie. This Oliver designed a <u>device</u> that makes sure you have clean flour in your bread. Watching the <u>production</u> of flour in 1780, Evans noticed that people were stepping on the grain at the mill, causing dirt to get into the flour. He began to look for <u>remedies</u> for the problem. Evans created an invention to move the grain automatically through the mill.

At first, few people <u>installed</u> Evans' invention in their mills. Evans' problem was not racial <u>discrimination</u>, for he was not a member of a minority. People just didn't want to try new ways of doing things. At last his idea was used, and today many kinds of factories are automated. Thanks to the <u>engineering</u> skill of Oliver Evans, dirt doesn't have to be one of the <u>ingredients</u> in your sandwich!

1. _____ put in place

2. _____ left without parents

3. _____ work of planning technical items

4. _____ instrument or tool

5. _____ prejudice in attitude or actions

6. _____ cures or corrections

7. _____ manufacturing

8. _____ items put into a mixture

Draw a picture of a funny invention that would help you do a job you don't like. Write a few sentences to tell about it.

Name _____

A. Before you read, complete the first two columns of the SQ3R chart. Complete the third column during and after reading.

SURVEY (page, heading)	QUESTION	READ, RECITE (answer)

B. Now REVIEW what you learned from reading. Write a few sentences to summarize the whole selection.

_____

_____

_____

A. Finish the sentences in these pictures. Add a helping verb on each line.

B. Write your own sentences for this picture. Use a helping verb and a main verb in each sentence.

Talking Tip

Tell a partner about an invention you wish you could make. Use at least two different helping verbs in your sentences.

Harcourt Brace School Publishers

Name _____

A. Welcome to the Museum of Inventions! Help prepare the labels for the museum's exhibits. Replace each number with a word from the list. Write the words on the lines below.

Do you ever have (1) keeping your ears warm? This invention by Chester Greenwood makes it (2) to have warm ears in the coldest weather.

When you drink clear, (3) water from one of these, it won't break like a glass (4). Hugh Moore developed paper cups in 1908 to help stop the spread of germs.

In 1863 James Plimpton made the first pair of roller skates that the wearer could steer, and (5) have been skating ever since.

You have probably used Earle Dickson's 1920 invention (6) times, especially if you've (7) and skinned your knee.

How many potato chips have you (8)? They were invented in 1853 by George Crum when he fried potato slices to a (9) brown. They had a very (10) crunch!

1. _____

2. _____

3. _____

4. _____

5. _____

bottle	eaten
people	golden
trouble	natural
fallen	several
special	possible

6. _____

7. _____

8. _____

9. _____

10. _____

B. Add vowels to these groups of letters to form words from the box.

11. hvn _____   14. rbbn _____

12. cntrl _____   15. lmn _____

13. lvn _____   16. lyl _____

central	eleven
heaven	lemon
loyal	ribbon

Harcourt Brace School Publishers

A. Read each question below. On the line, write the best reference source (or sources) for finding the answer. Choose from these four sources: *encyclopedia, dictionary, atlas,* **and** *globe.*

1. How far is it from Lynn, Massachusetts, to Boston? _____

2. How does a radio station transmitter work? _____

3. When did World War I take place? _____

4. What does *mortgage* mean? _____

5. When was the National Association for the Advancement of Colored People formed? _____

6. What countries border Suriname? _____

7. What is the correct pronunciation of *physics*? _____

8. How does an inventor apply for a patent? _____

9. What state is Philadelphia in? _____

10. Which syllable is accented in the word *inevitable*? _____

Harcourt Brace School Publishers

Name _____

B. Put yourself in the place of each student described below. Which reference sources would you use? Write *encyclopedia, dictionary, atlas,* or *globe* to answer each question. In some cases, your answer may include more than one.

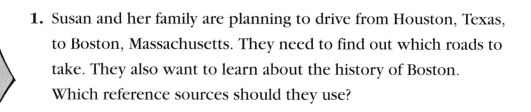

1. Susan and her family are planning to drive from Houston, Texas, to Boston, Massachusetts. They need to find out which roads to take. They also want to learn about the history of Boston. Which reference sources should they use?

   _____

2. Ahmad is preparing a social studies report about railroads in the United States. He needs more information, and he also needs to find the correct pronunciation of some of the parts of a train. Which reference sources should he use?

   _____

3. For a geography project, Carmen wants to find the place on the other side of the Earth that is exactly opposite her hometown. What reference source should she use?

   _____

4. Marcus needs to make a list of all the countries in South America. What reference sources could he use?

   _____

5. Jamie wants to find out exactly how a refrigeration unit works. What reference source should she use?

   _____

A. Read the following information. Summarize it on the sign below.

Benjamin Banneker, an African American, was a highly successful astronomer, farmer, mathematician, and surveyor. Born near Baltimore in 1731, Banneker learned to read and write from his grandmother. Attending a small school, he developed a deep interest in mathematics and science. In 1753, he built a clock made entirely from wood that he carved. It kept perfect time for over 50 years.

For five years starting in 1791, Banneker made all the weather predictions for a yearly almanac. He sent a copy of the book to Thomas Jefferson along with a letter calling for an end to slavery. Deeply impressed, Jefferson stepped up his own campaign against slavery. He also recommended Banneker to help lay out the boundaries for the District of Columbia.

_____

_____

_____

_____

_____

_____

_____

_____

Harcourt Brace School Publishers

Name _____

B. Read each quotation. Explain its meaning by paraphrasing it.

"Genius is 1 percent inspiration and 99 percent perspiration."

It means that _____

_____

_____.

"Necessity is the mother of invention."

It means that _____

_____

_____.

"Build a better mousetrap and the world will beat a path to your door."

It means that _____

_____

_____.

TRY THIS! Activity

Choose a poem, either one you already know or one that is new to you. Summarize the content of the poem in your own words. Share both the original poem and your summary with a classmate.

Harcourt Brace School Publishers

Use the words on the river to complete the outline.

century

descendant

I. Settlers want to _____ nature.

II. Industrial Revolution begins.

    A. Beginning of nineteenth _____ brings changes.

conquer

    B. _____ pollute water.

    C. Flow of _____ is _____ as paper pulp clogs river.

III. _____ of Weeawa starts cleanup.

chemicals

	c					
	o					
	n					
	q					
	u					
c	e	n	t	u	r	y
	r					

current

disrupted

TRY THIS! Word Play

Create a crossword puzzle that uses the words on the river. Add other words that will fit in the puzzle. Then trade puzzles with a classmate and solve each other's puzzle.

Name _____

A. Complete the time line below by writing story events in the boxes.

Time Line:
History of the Nashua River

Time Period		Event
Long ago (1400s)	⬇	Chief Weeawa's people settle by the Nashua River.
	⬇	
	⬇	
	⬇	
	⬇	
	⬇	
	⬇	
	⬇	

B. Use the information in your time line to write a brief story summary.

_____

_____

_____

_____

Harcourt Brace School Publishers

**A. Read the paragraph, and underline the verb in each sentence.
Then write *past*, *present*, or *future* above each verb to show its tense.**

We live near a beautiful stream. My mom fishes in the stream every weekend. Last

month she caught two big trout. They tasted terrific! My friends and I play in the

shallow water. Sometimes we swim in a deep pool in the stream. Next summer we

will float down the stream in inner tubes.

**B. Complete each sentence by writing a verb on the line. Use the
verb tense named in parentheses.**

1. Many tourists _____ the river. (present)

2. They _____ on the banks of the river. (present)

3. Last year a camera crew _____ to the river. (past)

4. They _____ a movie about the river. (past)

5. The movie _____ on TV next month. (future)

6. Everyone in town _____ it. (future)

TRY THIS!
Talking Tip

Tell a partner about a place you would like to visit. Use verbs in at least two different tenses.

Harcourt Brace School Publishers

Name _____

A. This artist is planning a display that will show an early American environment. Label each kind of animal, using words from the list. Write your answer on the line with the same number.

1. _____   5. _____

2. _____   6. _____

3. _____   7. _____

4. _____   8. _____

mice	deer
geese	calves
sheep	wolves
oxen	moose

B. Use a word from the list to complete each sentence or phrase.

9. Brush your _____.

10. _____ and husbands

11. They explored the universe in several _____.

12. forks and _____

13. _____ on the trees

14. _____ full of books

15. men and _____

16. programs for school-age _____

children
knives
leaves
shelves
spacecraft
teeth
wives
women

Harcourt Brace School Publishers

Use the picture and word clues to identify each word.

1. This word, from the Algonquian Indian language, names a soft leather slipper first worn by Native Americans.

Word: _____

2. This word, from the Algonquian *arakun,* literally means "scratcher."

Word: _____

3. This word, from the Sioux Indian language, names a cone-shaped tent used by Indians of the Great Plains.

Word: _____

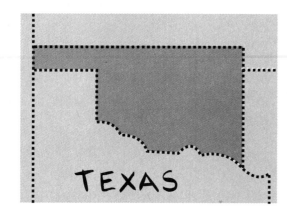

TEXAS

4. This word, from the Choctaw Indian language, names the state directly north of Texas.

Word: _____

Look on a map of the United States. See how many city, state, and river names you can find that come from Indian languages. You may use the dictionary for help. Compare your list with your classmates' lists.

Name _____

A. Read each passage. Then synthesize the important information on the lines below.

1. The Mississippi River is the longest river in the United States. It flows all the way from Minnesota to the Gulf of Mexico. It is the nation's chief inland waterway. Ships carry agricultural goods, industrial products, and raw materials along its route.

2. During the 1500s, the Mississippi River provided a route for Spanish explorers. Later, in the 1600s, French explorers relied on it as well. In the 1800s, the river became an important transportation route for the newly developed steamboat.

_____

_____

_____

_____

_____

_____

GO ON

B. Think of a subject you are interested in. Think about two books, movies, or television shows on that subject, and list some of the important ideas found in each. Then on the lines below, synthesize the information from the two sources.

Source: _____

Ideas: _____

_____

_____

Source: _____

Ideas: _____

_____

_____

Synthesized information: _____

_____

_____

_____

_____

_____

TRY THIS!
Learning Log

Explain the steps you follow to synthesize information. Then tell why synthesizing is an important skill in writing a research report.

Name _____

Write the entry word or words you would look up in an encyclopedia for each of the following situations.

1. You want to learn the exact location of the Nashua River.

   Entry: _____

2. You want to learn how a river is formed.

   Entry: _____

3. You want to learn how Native Americans used rivers to their advantage.

   Entry: _____

4. You want to learn about pollution of our rivers and skies.

   Entry: _____

5. You want to learn more about Lynne Cherry, author of the book *A River Ran Wild.*

   Entry: _____

Look at different headlines in a newspaper. Decide what encyclopedia listing could help you find out more information on the topic of each newspaper article. Compare your answers with a classmate's.

Name _____

Read the following letter. Summarize and paraphrase the information.

Dear Phoebe,

I just got a new job working in a cloth factory. The factory overlooks the Nashua River, but we have to keep our windows closed because the river smells terrible!

My job is to cut the cloth that the weavers make. Other workers dye the cloth beautiful colors. Last week, they were using purple dyes. The river was purple for a whole week as they dumped the old dyes into the water. The week before, they were using yellow dyes. Guess what color the water was then!

My mom told me that the river used to be clear. She says there used to be a lot of fish in it, and lots of animals came to its banks. It's hard to believe. I wonder if this river will ever be clean again.

Your friend,

Alice

Dear Phoebe,

_____

_____

_____

_____

Your friend,

Alice

TRY THIS! Activity

Choose an article from a newspaper or magazine. Summarize and paraphrase the main information in the article. Share it with classmates.

Harcourt Brace School Publishers

Name _____

Welcome to the planet Pollooton! Complete the cartoon by writing a word from the list on each line.

millennium   chain reactions   haze

oppression   endangered

Our planet is in a mess! We can hardly see because the _____ makes everything look foggy.

Not many of us are left. We are all _____. To survive, we must fight the _____ of the evil King Pollooton!

Cleaner air . . . cleaner water . . . a better place to live! We'll start some cleanup _____!

Come back to see us in another _____ and see how clean everything is!

Create a weird science fiction cartoon of your own. Use at least one of the vocabulary words in your characters' conversation.

A. Add details to the Cause-Effect Diagram.

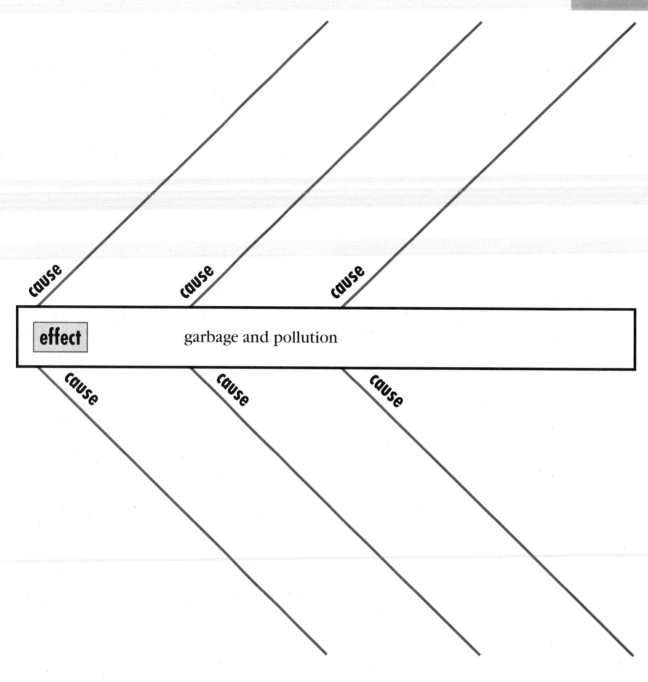

cause

cause

cause

| effect | garbage and pollution |

cause

cause

cause

B. What do you feel is the message of the selection?

_____

_____

_____

Harcourt Brace School Publishers

Name _____

A. Complete each sentence. Write the past-tense form of the verb in parentheses.

1. Someone _____ a sandwich wrapper. (drop)

2. Another person _____ a can onto the ground. (toss)

3. People _____ all of this pollution. (cause)

4. We _____ up the park. (clean)

5. Many helpers _____ together. (work)

B. Complete each sentence in this poster. Write the present-tense form of the verb in parentheses.

Pollution _____ everyone. (hurt)

It _____ the world dirty. (make)

Children _____ clean air and water. (need)

People _____ happier in clean places. (feel)

We _____ a pollution-free planet. (want)

TRY THIS! Writing

Make your own poster that encourages people to clean up an area of your school or community. In your poster, use present-tense verbs and past-tense verbs in sentences to add to your message.

A. These time travelers have arrived in the twenty-third century, and they're having trouble reading this message. In place of each mixed-up word, find a word from the list that makes sense. Write the words on the lines below.

We hope you have come in (1) XFQLM and will not hurt us. Who has (2) ZLPR you to us? When your (3) JKPRZ landed on the flat (4) SRWTQ outside the city, we did not know if we could talk with you. Now that we have (5) RQTLK you speak, we know you can understand our language. Please help us learn how to use our resources carefully and not (6) LPTRB them. We want to stop polluting and smell the (7) WRTPL of flowers. Please (8) WRZPF your silence and give us a (9) KLPMC of advice!

1. _____   4. _____   7. _____

2. _____   5. _____   8. _____

3. _____   6. _____   9. _____

plane	plain
heard	piece
sent	break
peace	waste
scent	

B. Answer each riddle with a rhyme. Use words from the list.

10. What's a penny that's been used to buy something? a spent _____

11. What could you call a group of sparrows? a bird _____

12. What are two rectangles, each with four equal sides? a square _____

13. What would you have if you tied a long shoelace around your middle? a laced _____

herd	cent	pear	brake
	pair	waist	pare

14. What pedal stops a rattler or python? a snake _____

15–16. What happens when you remove the peel from an unusual fruit? You _____ a rare _____.

Name _____

Write each of the following slang expressions in more formal language.

These wheels are cool!

_____
_____
_____

I'll show them I'm no chicken!

_____
_____
_____

Bummer! I just totaled my plane.

_____
_____
_____

This hot weather is driving me up a wall!

_____
_____
_____

TRY THIS!
Talking Tip

Slang is acceptable in informal situations but not in formal ones. Tell a friend about your weekend. Use slang expressions. Then have your friend describe the same weekend to you, using formal language.

A. Read the details in each web. Use the information to make a generalization.

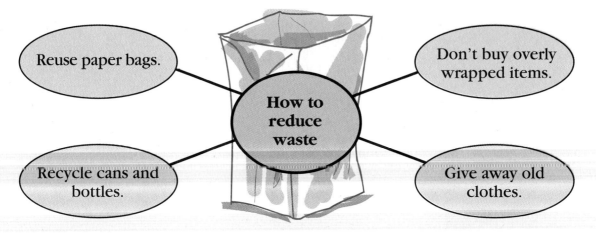

Reuse paper bags.

Don't buy overly wrapped items.

How to reduce waste

Recycle cans and bottles.

Give away old clothes.

Generalization: _____

Garbage pollutes rivers.

Gas fumes pollute air.

Sources of pollution

Toxic waste pollutes soil.

Smoke and fumes pollute sky.

Generalization: _____

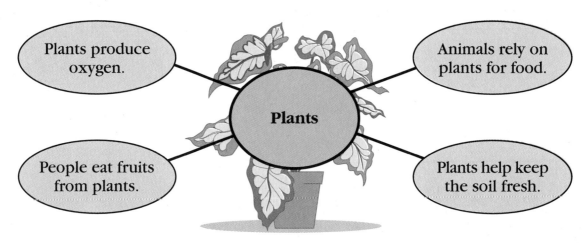

Plants produce oxygen.

Animals rely on plants for food.

Plants

People eat fruits from plants.

Plants help keep the soil fresh.

Generalization: _____

Harcourt Brace School Publishers

Name _____

B. Read each generalization. Write three details that could support the generalization.

1. Rules help guarantee a safe society.

   Detail 1: _____

   Detail 2: _____

   Detail 3: _____

2. Having a good education is important.

   Detail 1: _____

   Detail 2: _____

   Detail 3: _____

3. Animals play a key role in our world.

   Detail 1: _____

   Detail 2: _____

   Detail 3: _____

TRY THIS!
Learning Log

How do you make a generalization? Describe the steps that you follow. Then tell how making generalizations can be helpful when reading a social studies article.

SCIENCE Write the volume number you would use to find
information on each of the following science topics.

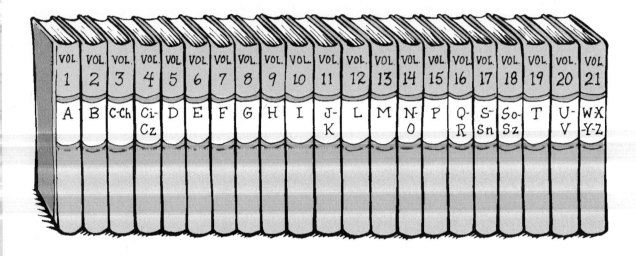

_____ **1.** life cycle of a butterfly

_____ **2.** different types of cancer

_____ **3.** parts of a flower

_____ **4.** habitats of snakes

_____ **5.** Albert Einstein's work

_____ **6.** reasons for the dinosaur's extinction

_____ **7.** uses of radium

_____ **8.** rain forest plants and animals

_____ **9.** Alexander Graham Bell's inventions

_____ **10.** how copper is produced

TRY THIS!
Activity

Write ten statements that you find in different volumes of an encyclopedia.
Read each statement to a classmate. See if the classmate can guess the name of
the article that contains the statement.

Name _____

Use the words on the flags to complete the story below.

distinguished   **splendid**   **composed**

delicate   **monotony**   **constantly**

artificial

Once upon a time, a lovely princess lived in a _____

castle. Because the princess loved music, her father, the king, hired the

most famous and _____ musician he could find to teach

the princess to play the harp. She practiced _____ and

learned quickly. Every day, she _____ beautiful songs as

her _____ fingers flew over the harp strings. On a chain

she even wore a small harp carved from an _____

diamond that looked like a real one.

After many months, the princess

grew tired of harp music. "Day after

day, it's always the same," she said. "I'm

tired of this _____. I

need a change. I want to play guitar in

a rock band!"

And that is just what she did.

Can you imagine life as a prince or princess? Try writing a short, silly fairy tale of your own.
Use at least two of the vocabulary words.

TRY THIS!
Writing

Harcourt Brace School Publishers

A. One way to summarize a story is to complete a Problem-Solution Map. Use the map below.

Problem

Solution

Problem

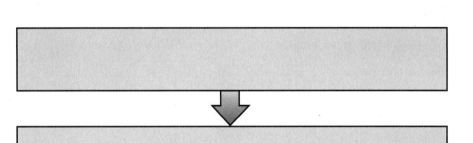

Solution

Problem

Solution

Final Outcome

B. What do you think the Emperor learns by the end of the story?

_____

_____

_____

Name _____

A. Complete each sentence by writing the past-tense form of the verb in parentheses.

1. We _____ a tiny bird. (see)

2. A beautiful song _____ from its throat. (come)

3. I got out my camera and _____ a picture. (take)

4. I _____, "I want to know more about this bird." (think)

5. I _____ to my friend, "Let's follow that bird." (say)

6. My friend and I _____ after the bird. (run)

7. We _____ as fast as we could. (go)

8. The bird _____ us one last song and then flew away. (give)

B. Write two sentences of your own, telling what happened next. In one of your sentences, use the past-tense form of the verb *drive, ride,* **or** *do.*

_____

_____

_____

_____

_____

_____

_____

TRY THIS! Game

Make your own crossword puzzle using the past-tense forms of at least six irregular verbs. Outline the spaces on graph paper, or draw squares on lined paper. Number the first space of each word. Then write present-tense verbs as clues to the puzzle. Let a classmate try to solve your puzzle.

**A. Complete the royal sign-maker's poster. Write a word
from the list that has the same or almost the same
meaning as each word or group of words in parentheses.**

cheerful	payment	sadness
priceless	awful	hopeless
agreement	grateful	happiness
useless	illness	movement

Attention, all people of the empire!

*The Emperor is suffering from a terrible (sickness) _____. He
believes that listening to (joyful) _____ music and watching the graceful
(act of moving) _____ of dancers will make him feel much better.*

*Doctors say that the Emperor's condition is almost (without hope)
_____ and anything we do may be (not helpful at all)
_____. However, the Emperor does not agree with this (terrible)
_____ prediction. He and the Empress are in (a state of thinking the
same) _____ that music and dance would bring him much (pleasure)
_____ and would help end his (gloom) _____!*

*Anyone who can cheer the Emperor with music and dance will receive a (very
valuable) _____ reward. The (thankful) _____ Emperor
will be glad to make a large (money that is given) _____ to the person
who can make him well.*

**B. These base words and suffixes are all mixed
up! In place of each incorrect suffix, add the one
needed to form a word from the list. Write the
word on the line.**

careless	endless
wonderful	colorful

1. wonderless _____

2. colorness _____   3. endful _____   4. careness _____

Name _____

Write the meaning of each homograph. Use the word in a sentence.

box

Meaning: _____

Sentence: _____

Meaning: _____

Sentence: _____

wind

Meaning: _____

Sentence: _____

Meaning: _____

Sentence: _____

pen

Meaning: _____

Sentence: _____

Meaning: _____

Sentence: _____

bow

Meaning: _____

Sentence: _____

Meaning: _____

Sentence: _____

Give your partner the meanings for two homographs. For example: "This word can refer to the flow of water or to something up-to-date. What's the word?" *(current)* See if your partner can guess the homographs.

Name _____

A. For each pair of things below, list three ways the two are similar. Then list three ways they are different.

 a bird and an airplane

Likenesses		Differences	

 a penny and a nickel

Likenesses		Differences	

a pencil and a pen

Likenesses		Differences	

Name _____

B. Choose two animals. Draw a sketch of each animal below. Then list four ways the animals are alike and four ways they are different.

Likenesses   Differences

1. _____   1. _____

2. _____   2. _____

3. _____   3. _____

4. _____   4. _____

Now choose two foods and draw each below. List four ways the foods are similar and four ways they are different.

Likenesses   Differences

1. _____   1. _____

2. _____   2. _____

3. _____   3. _____

4. _____   4. _____

TRY THIS! Learning Log

How can you tell in a reading selection when two things are being compared? How can you tell when they are being contrasted? Why is understanding comparison and contrast an important skill when reading a science article? Write your answers.

Name _____

Robby is telling about his painting. Fill in the missing words.
The words you need are on the brushes.

impressions   omit   exhibition   prodigies   inspiration   effects   stimulates

I'm finishing this painting for a museum _____.

I looked at a sunset and then painted my _____ of it.

I was planning to include a tree, but I decided to _____ it.

I use different colors to create different _____.

Everything I see is an _____ for my painting.

Some child _____ do nothing but paint, but I like to play soccer, too. Exercise _____ my mind!

TRY THIS! Activity

Choose one of the words on the brushes, and use a dictionary to find its definition. Your definition should not be longer than ten words. Copy the definition on a strip of paper, and then cut the words apart. Ask a classmate to put the words in order so the definition makes sense.

Name _____

A. Complete the Story Impressions Chart.

Story Impressions Chart

Story Impressions	Story
amazing talent ⬇ learned by doing ⬇ own pace ⬇ father ⬇ guidance and support	

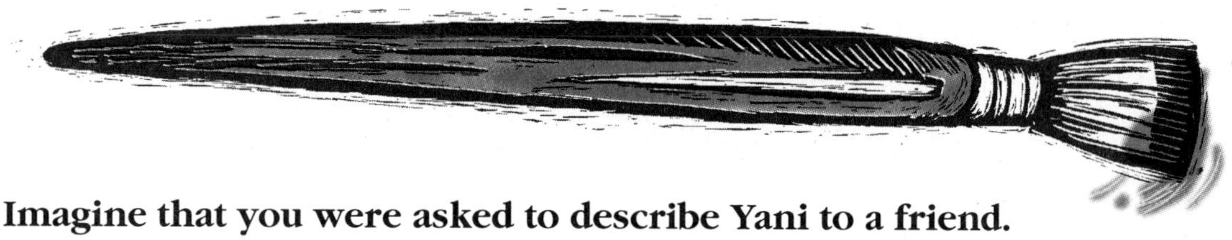

B. Imagine that you were asked to describe Yani to a friend. Write what you would say.

_____

_____

_____

Harcourt Brace School Publishers

A. Read the sentences in the picture. Underline the verbs that are in the future tense.

B. Write your own sentences to answer these questions. Use a future-tense verb in each sentence.

1. What will you do later today?

_____

2. What do you hope to do with your friends tomorrow?

_____

3. What are you planning to do next summer?

_____

4. What do you think you will be doing ten years from now?

_____

Write your answers to these questions.
- What does a verb in the future tense describe?
- How do you form the future tense of a verb?

Harcourt Brace School Publishers

Name _____

A. These artists are speaking to young painters. Complete their advice by writing words from the list where they belong.

> basket   master   hidden   picnic   public
> ugly   problem   sudden   temper   wallet

Be willing to try. You may discover _____ talents that you never knew you had!

Practice painting everyday objects. My first painting was of a _____ of food packed to go on a _____.

Don't lose your _____ and throw away work because you think it looks _____. All of a _____, you may find you are able to solve the _____.

Don't give up. It takes years to _____ the skills of painting. If a private or _____ museum buys one of your paintings, it could mean a lot of money in your _____!

B. Write words from the list to finish this description.

batter
copper
ladder
puppet
rabbit
silver

My latest work is a painting of a country kitchen. A table holds a bowl of cake _____. The spoon is not gleaming _____ or even _____. It is carved from wood. The entire wall is covered with shelves, with a _____ for reaching those at the top. Supplies are stored there, along with a child's doll, a stuffed toy _____, and a hand _____.

SPELLING: SPELLING PATTERNS: VCCV WORDS   **159**

Write a synonym and an antonym for each underlined word.

tired

Synonym: _____

Antonym: _____

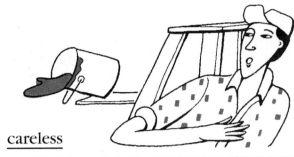

careless

Synonym: _____

Antonym: _____

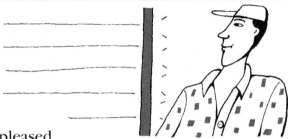

pleased

Synonym: _____

Antonym: _____

beautiful

Synonym: _____

Antonym: _____

finished

Synonym: _____

Antonym: _____

slanted

Synonym: _____

Antonym: _____

TRY THIS! Game

Think of a word. Tell your partner a synonym and an antonym for the word. See if the partner can guess the word. If the guess is wrong, offer another synonym and antonym.

Name _____

A. Write whether each statement below is a *fact* or an *opinion*. Circle the words that signal an opinion.

_____ 1. Yani was painting pictures of cats and monkeys at the age of three.

_____ 2. Her earliest paintings probably do not reflect her best work.

_____ 3. Yani's father is also a painter who has given his daughter advice from time to time.

_____ 4. Yani has had her work exhibited in many cities in China.

_____ 5. Yani is perhaps too modest about her paintings.

_____ 6. In the future, Yani's paintings will almost certainly be considered the best works of art in China.

_____ 7. Yani paints all her pictures from memory.

_____ 8. A painting of a bridge is usually not pleasing to the eye.

_____ 9. Yani's artistic views do not always agree with her father's.

_____ 10. Yani's father is too strict in his treatment of his daughter.

GO ON

**B. Read the following letter that Yani wrote. Draw a line under
each fact. Circle each opinion.**

Dear Suki,

    I just returned from a tour of seven cities. They were the best
places in all of China! My paintings were on exhibit in each city. My
father traveled with me the entire time. He is wonderful company for
a long trip. I met many other painters during my travels. They told me
about their attitudes toward painting. Their work is really
interesting.

                 Sincerely,
                 Yani

**Now write a brief letter that Suki might send to Yani. Underline
each fact, and circle each opinion.**

Explain how you can tell the difference between a fact and an opinion. Why is it important to be
able to tell the difference when you read?

Name _____

Read the following two paragraphs. Then fill in the Venn diagram below with ways that the subjects are alike and different.

Michelangelo, who lived from 1475 to 1564, is one of the best-known artists of all time. As a leading artist during the period called the Italian Renaissance, Michelangelo was interested mainly in creating large marble statues. His varied talents also led him to produce great paintings and even poetry. Michelangelo focused on the human body in much of his work. His subjects also were often characters from the Bible.

Leonardo Da Vinci was one of the most famous painters in the world. He was a key figure during the Italian Renaissance. Da Vinci, who lived from 1452 to 1519, was trained to be a painter, but he achieved greatness in other fields as well, including anatomy, astronomy, botany, and geology. He designed many machines and drew plans for hundreds of inventions.

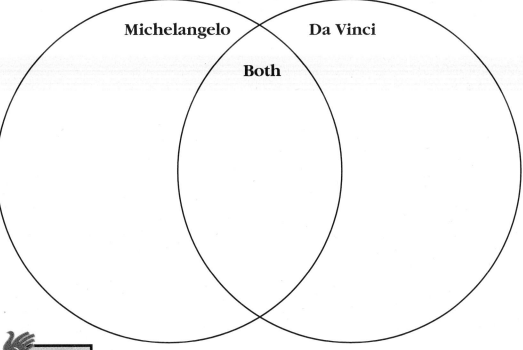

Michelangelo　　　　**Da Vinci**

Both

Find two different pictures in a book or magazine. List several ways that the pictures are alike. Then list ways that they are different. Share your lists. See if a classmate can find more similarities and differences.

Harcourt Brace School Publishers

**Read each paragraph. Write
a generalization that you can
make from the information.**

Many Chinese paintings have birds as their subject, while others show
flowers. Other Chinese artwork includes landscapes of the countryside,
the mountains, and the sea.

Generalization: _____

_____

Raphael, who lived in the 1500s, was a popular Italian painter known
for his balanced, appealing designs. Another famous Italian artist was
Michelangelo, whose paintings on the ceiling of the Sistine Chapel in
Rome are well known.

Generalization: _____

_____

A major movement in art, called romanticism, developed in France in
the early 1800s. In the mid-1800s, a movement called realism took over.
Later, in the late 1800s, a movement called impressionism developed.

Generalization: _____

_____

Invite two classmates to tell you about several activities they enjoy. From the
information, see what generalizations you can make about their interests and
talents.

Harcourt Brace School Publishers

Name _____

Use the clues to decide where in the puzzle to write each word. The words you need are on the pots.

chisel   legends   traditional   culture   potters   kiln   cylinders

ACROSS

1. Cans of food are different sizes of these.
2. They create figures from clay.
3. It's an oven for firing pottery.

DOWN

1. It's a tool for cutting and shaping.
4. This word describes something that people have done the same way for a long time.
5. These are stories that have come down from earlier times.
6. This is the way of life of a people.

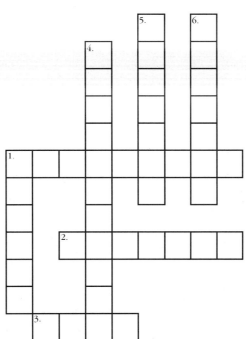

Try some fancy writing. Choose one of the vocabulary words, and write it in a way that shows its meaning. For example, you might turn the *o* in *potter* into a pot. See how many of the words you can illustrate this way.

potter

Name ___________________________

A. **Complete the flowcharts by listing the steps in each process.**

Pottery	**Cochiti Drum**
↓	↓
↓	↓
↓	↓
↓	

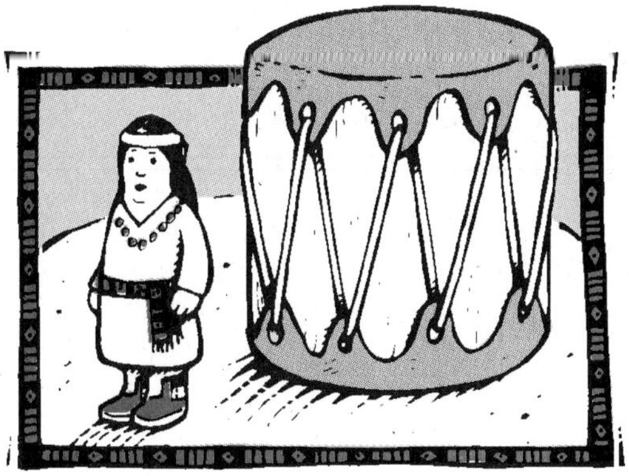

B. **Summarize the main idea of the selection.**

____

____

____

Name _____

Imagine that you are famous for the clay pots and figures you make. An interviewer has come to ask you questions about your work. Write a sentence with an adverb to answer each question. Choose adverbs from the box, or think of your own adverbs.

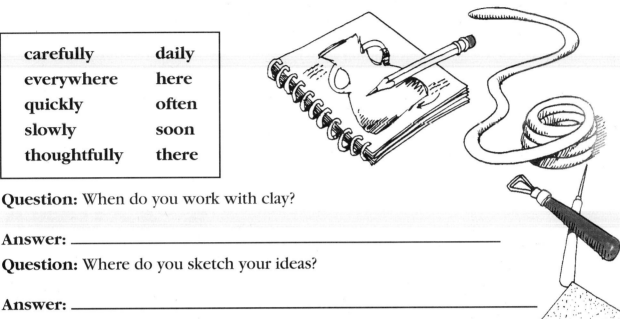

carefully	daily
everywhere	here
quickly	often
slowly	soon
thoughtfully	there

Question: When do you work with clay?

Answer: _____

Question: Where do you sketch your ideas?

Answer: _____

Question: How do you draw your sketches?

Answer: _____

Question: How do you roll the clay?

Answer: _____

Question: How do you sand your finished works?

Answer: _____

Question: Where is your work on display?

Answer: _____

Question: When will you be interviewed again?

Answer: _____

Write the sentence starter *I can move* _____ on three slips of paper. Write a different adverb on each slip to finish the sentence. Then form a group with three or four classmates. Mix all the sentences together. Take turns choosing one sentence and acting it out. See if the other group members can guess the adverb.

Harcourt Brace School Publishers

A. Unscramble each group of letters to form a word from the list. Write the word on the line.

1. fafcrit _____

2. clipsat _____

3. magrram _____

4. gabreag _____

5. tropra _____

6. nenlut _____

plastic	parrot
grammar	tunnel
traffic	garbage

B. Monica and her grandmother enjoy telling each other stories. Complete the titles of the stories they have created. (Hint: Don't forget to capitalize each word!)

blanket lesson perfect harvest thunder
cannon contest pattern surface squirrel

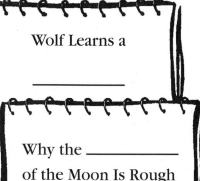

Wolf Learns a

_____

Why the _____
of the Moon Is Rough

Grandmother Weaves

a Woolen _____

Why _____

Booms Like a

_____

A _____ Sunny

Day

Sparrow and Robin

Have a Weaving

_____

The Pot with the

Zigzag _____

Mouse Gets Ready to

_____ the Grain

Why _____

Hides Nuts for the

Winter

Name _____

Write the meaning of each pottery-making word below. Then use the word in a sentence of your own. Use a dictionary if you need help.

1. kiln

Meaning: _____

Sentence: _____

_____

2. potter

Meaning: _____

Sentence: _____

_____

3. earthenware

Meaning: _____

Sentence: _____

_____

4. potter's wheel

Meaning: _____

Sentence: _____

_____

Pantomime a word that is related to pottery making. Challenge a classmate to guess the word. Then try to guess your classmate's word.

A. Read each passage. Identify whether it is written in *first-person* or *third-person* point of view. Underline the pronouns that help you know.

1. The children danced together during Pueblo Feast Day. First, they listened as the singer chanted his song and the drummer banged her drum. Then they began to move in rhythm, acting out the story through their motions.

   Point of View: _____

2. My father and I stopped at the village. We saw some storyteller dolls on a shelf. An Indian woman handed one of the dolls to me. I thought the doll was very beautiful. The woman told us to keep it as a gift.

   Point of View: _____

B. Rewrite each passage above from the opposite point of view.

1. _____

   _____

   _____

   _____

2. _____

   _____

   _____

   _____

Explain how you can tell whether a story is written in first-person or third-person point of view. What are the advantages of reading a story told from each point of view?

Harcourt Brace School Publishers

Name _____

Read the following information. Then list similarities and differences between the Hopi Indians and the Zuni Indians.

The Hopi Indians are a part of the Pueblo Indian tribes. The Hopi live primarily on reservations in northeastern Arizona. They dwell in villages near high tablelands, or mesas. One of their villages, about 800 years old, is among the oldest Indian villages in the United States that are still occupied. Like their ancestors, the Hopi of today raise sheep and grow crops. They also make and sell baskets, pottery, jewelry, and dolls.

The Zuni Indians live in northwestern New Mexico, near the Arizona border. They are a part of the Pueblo Indian tribes. Many Zuni live in adobe and stone houses in pueblo villages. The Zuni are famous for jewelry that they make from silver, turquoise, and coral. They also raise livestock, as did many of their ancestors. Zuni villages were first discovered by foreigners in 1539.

Similarities	Differences

Choose two characters in stories your class has read. Describe the ways they are alike. Then describe how they are different. Share your descriptions with a classmate. See if the classmate can guess who the two characters are.

Read each sentence about "The Skirt." Then answer the question with a complete sentence of your own that uses the underlined word.

 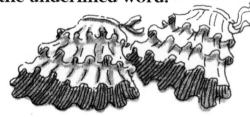

1. Miata wears her hair <u>coiled</u> into a bun. What other things might be coiled?

_____

_____

2. Miata liked her old skirt well enough to <u>rescue</u> it. What are some other things that are sometimes rescued?

_____

_____

3. A stiff skirt can <u>rustle</u>. What else might rustle?

_____

_____

4. Miata <u>ignores</u> what her brother says. What do you sometimes ignore?

_____

_____

5. The lace on the skirt <u>ripples</u> in the light. What else might ripple?

_____

_____

TRY THIS! Activity

The sound of the word *rustle* reminds you of its meaning. Make a list of other words, such as *buzz*, that sound like what they mean. Compare lists with a classmate.

Harcourt Brace School Publishers

Name _____

A. Complete the Prediction Chart.

Prediction Chart

What I Predict Will Happen	What Actually Happened

B. Describe Miata's problem and how she solves it.

_____

_____

_____

_____

A. Read the following paragraph, and underline each adverb that compares. Also underline any word that helps an adverb make a comparison.

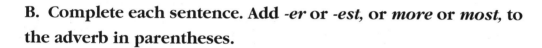

The dance performance was a great success, and we all felt like stars. Leo, one of the new dancers, leaped higher than anyone else. Shelley twirled faster than Gemma, but Nikki twirled the fastest of all. In her solo, Ella moved more gracefully than she had ever moved before. When we took our curtain calls, Kai bowed lower than anyone else. Of all the people in the audience, my brother clapped the most enthusiastically.

B. Complete each sentence. Add *-er* or *-est*, or *more* or *most*, to the adverb in parentheses.

1. Antonio practices _____ than anyone else in the dance group. (long)

2. Of all the dancers, he works the _____. (hard)

3. Anya misses rehearsals _____ than I do. (often)

4. Ms. Chyu reminds us to warm up _____ than we dance. (slowly)

5. She works the _____ of all our teachers. (patiently)

TRY THIS!
Talking Tip

Tell a partner about a sports event you have watched. Tell how several athletes did in that event. Use at least two adverbs that compare.

Harcourt Brace School Publishers

Name _____

A. Complete the poster by writing a word from the list in place of each number. Write the words on the lines.

Dance (1) Hits School!
Dancers Needed for Cultural Heritage Day

Cultural Heritage Day, April 19, will (2) on the songs and dances of Latin America. Male and (3) dancers are needed for the celebration. If you have ever been a (4) in a dance class, or if you just love to dance, please come on Friday at 3 P.M. to try out. Dancers will be needed for next month's celebration and for those in the (5), too. Don't just stand there in (6). Share the (7) and excitement of Latin American culture! There will be free (8) for thirsty dancers!

 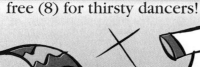   

1. _____   5. _____

2. _____   6. _____

3. _____   7. _____

4. _____   8. _____

fever	female
soda	pupil
future	beauty
silence	focus

B. Create words from the list by filling in the missing vowel–consonant–vowel in the middle of each group of letters below. Write the words on the lines.

cedar
legal
meters
pilot
pirate
polar
solar
tiger

9. m ___ rs _____   13. c ___ r _____

10. p ___ r _____   14. l ___ l _____

11. p ___ te _____   15. s ___ r _____

12. t ___ r _____   16. p ___ t _____

SPELLING: SPELLING PATTERNS: VCV WORDS **175**

A. Read each sentence below. Find words and phrases that appeal to the five senses. Record each word or phrase in the chart below.

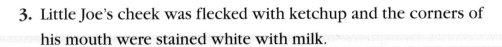

1. The radio in the kitchen was softly playing Mexican songs.

2. Miata's mother sipped hot coffee and ate a spicy tortilla.

3. Little Joe's cheek was flecked with ketchup and the corners of his mouth were stained white with milk.

4. When Mother patted Miata's hand, Miata opened her eyes.

5. The shiny lace rippled in the light.

6. Miata liked the bright new colors and the fresh smell.

Sight	Hearing	Taste

Smell	Touch

Name _____

B. For each picture below, write a sentence that appeals to the sense that is given.

Appeal to taste: _____

_____

Appeal to sound: _____

_____

Appeal to touch: _____

_____

Appeal to smell: _____

_____

Appeal to sight: _____

_____

TRY THIS! Learning Log

Explain how descriptive language, or imagery, can help you appreciate what you read. How does it help you better understand what the characters experience?

A. Read the following letter to the editor. Underline each fact. Circle each opinion.

Dear Editor:

The students in our school should wear uniforms. Many kids in this school put too much emphasis on how they look. Some students come from families that do not have a lot of money. Every day they see many of their classmates dressed in expensive outfits. That has to make them feel bad.

School is a place to learn. Worrying about how you look is not part of the learning process. If we wore uniforms, everyone would be dressed the same way. No one would have to plan what to wear in the morning. It would be fairer and easier for everyone if we had a uniform dress code.

Sincerely,

A Concerned Student

Write one more fact the letter writer could have added.

_____

_____

Write one more opinion the letter writer could have added.

_____

_____

Harcourt Brace School Publishers

Name _____

B. Read each fact or opinion. Fill in the balloon next to it with a fact or opinion on the same topic.

Facts	**Opinions**

Mexico City, with more than ten million people, is the largest city in the world.

Mexican food is very tasty.

Mexican children play the piñata game by breaking a toy animal filled with treats.

The Rio Grande is the most beautiful river in the world.

With a partner, read a newspaper advertisement. First, identify the facts in the ad. Then, identify the opinions.

Harcourt Brace School Publishers

Read each word and its definition. Then join Shane and Carla at a dance performance. Complete each sentence by choosing one of the words and writing it on the line.

Word	Definition
rhythm	the repeating beat of music
tempo	speed of the beat of a dance or piece of music
choreography	planned set of dance movements
jubilation	great gladness or happiness
heritage	traditions handed down from the past
debut	first public performance
dignity	honor; pride; self-respect

"The program says this dance group has never performed before. It's their _____," said Carla.

Shane read his program. "It says their dances celebrate their Native American _____," he said.

"The first dance is a slow one. It shows the _____ of their people."

"I like dances with a fast _____ the best," said Carla.

"I feel the _____ and want to dance, too."

"Then you'll like the second dance," Shane told her.

"The program says the dancers will use fast movements to show their feeling of _____."

"I wish I could plan _____ like that," Carla answered.

Writing

What kind of dance do you like best? Create an invitation to a performance of that type of dance. Make it as colorful as you like, and use at least two of the vocabulary words.

Harcourt Brace School Publishers

Name _____

A. Read the Anticipation Guide. If the statement is true, write *True* on the line below. If the statement is false, rewrite it so it becomes true.

Anticipation Guide

1. Alvin Ailey became a famous choreographer.

_____

2. Alvin Ailey started to study dance when he was 30.

_____

3. He learned to dance on his own.

_____

4. He created a dance performance called *Blues Suite*.

_____

5. The first performance he choreographed was not very successful.

_____

6. He drew upon his African American heritage to create his dances.

_____

7. Many of his dances were done to traditional ballet music.

_____

B. Briefly describe how Alvin Ailey rose to success as a dancer and choreographer.

_____

_____

_____

Flip and Flop don't agree about anything! Read each sentence Flip says. Then change the sentence by using a negative. Write the changed sentence in Flop's speech balloon.

With a partner, make up four more pairs of sentences that Flip and Flop might say. Take turns saying a sentence that does not have a negative. Then change the sentence by using a negative.

Name _____

A. Write words from the list where they belong in the dancers' conversation.

easy	music	student	basic	native
duties	major	eager	patient	humor

I began learning the most _____ steps of ballet when I was five. I thought, "There's nothing to this! It's _____!" I was wrong. I have had to be very _____ and practice each step many times.

I'm a _____ of Mexico, and that's where I first learned to dance. Now one of my _____ is to plan the important, _____ performances of a large dance company.

Ever since I was a child, I've loved to move to _____. By the time I was a fourth-grade _____, I was _____ to take dance lessons. I've learned to perform dances that are serious and dances that are full of _____.

B. Write the word from the list that each phrase makes you think of.

1. a breakfast treat _____

2. a sticky tag _____

3. a toothy animal _____

4. something to use for measuring _____

5. really great _____

6. trees and flowers _____

bacon
beaver
label
nature
ruler
super

**Write the meaning of each music word below. Then use the word
in an original sentence. Use a dictionary for help, if you like.**

1. staff

Meaning: _____

Sentence: _____

_____

2. baton

Meaning: _____

Sentence: _____

_____

3. conductor

Meaning: _____

Sentence: _____

_____

4. note

Meaning: _____

Sentence: _____

_____

Make a list of several words that relate to music or dance. Write a sentence using each word.
Read the sentence to a classmate, saying "blank" in place of the word. See how many words your
classmate can guess correctly. Then try to guess your classmate's words.

Name _____

Write two possible meanings for each word below. Then place a ✓ next to one of your meanings. Write a sentence that uses the word according to that meaning. Include context clues.

1. glasses

Meaning 1: _____

Meaning 2: _____

Sentence: _____

2. company

Meaning 1: _____

Meaning 2: _____

Sentence: _____

3. stick

Meaning 1: _____

Meaning 2: _____

Sentence: _____

4. channel

Meaning 1: _____

Meaning 2: _____

Sentence: _____

TRY THIS! Learning Log

Explain how you use context clues in a sentence to determine the meaning of a multiple-meaning word. Tell why it's important to know which meaning of the word applies.

Read the dance review below. Identify each numbered sentence as a *simile* or a *metaphor.* Then explain what the sentence means.

NEW YORK CITY—(1) The newest dance company to perform in New York arrived like a tornado at the Broadway Theater last night. The Movement Masters gave a lively first performance. (2) The dancers were like energized grasshoppers, leaping all over the stage. The audience loudly applauded each solo. (3) Each performer was a powerful firecracker exploding on the wide wooden platform. Dancers spun, dipped, looped, and somersaulted. (4) At the end of the show, the audience was an applause machine unwilling to turn off. The clapping went on for several minutes. Finally, the director took one final bow. (5) The moment was like a beautiful sunset.

1. _____

_____

2. _____

_____

3. _____

_____

4. _____

_____

5. _____

_____

Read a newspaper or magazine review of a program of music, dance, or theater or of an art exhibit. See how many similes and metaphors you can locate in the article. Then choose other sentences from the review and rewrite them as similes or metaphors, without changing the meaning.

Harcourt Brace School Publishers

Name _____

Read each statement below. Write whether it is a *fact* or an *opinion*. If it is a fact, write a related statement that is an opinion. If it is an opinion, write a related statement that is a fact.

1. Alvin Ailey is the best African American dancer who ever lived.

   _____

   _____

2. Ailey created his own steps as he studied dance. _____

   _____

   _____

3. Ailey was wise to form his own dance company. _____

   _____

   _____

4. Ailey's dance company performed *Blues Suite* in their first public

   appearance. _____

   _____

5. All future dancers will be influenced in some way by Alvin Ailey.

   _____

   _____

Choose a subject, such as sports or music. Write five facts about the subject. Then invite a classmate to write five opinions, each relating to one of your facts.

Harcourt Brace School Publishers

SKILLS AND STRATEGIES INDEX

VOCABULARY

Analogies 81

Compound words 121

Connotation/denotation 14

Content-area vocabulary 7

Descriptive words 65

Homographs 153

Homophones 27

Key words 3, 10, 17, 23, 31, 38, 47, 55, 61, 69, 77, 85, 94, 101, 110, 117, 124, 132, 141, 149, 156, 165, 172, 180

Native American words 136

Spanish words 105

Specialized vocabulary 169

   Music words 184

   Slang 145

Synonyms 89

Synonyms and antonyms 35, 160

Words from different languages 42

COMPREHENSION

Cause and effect 66-67, 75, 84

Comparing and contrasting 154-155, 163, 171

Connotation and denotation 106-107

Context clues 98-99, 108, 116

Expository text 73-74, 92-93

Fact and opinion 161-162, 178-179, 187

Main idea and details 90-91, 109, 115

Making generalizations 146-147, 164

Making judgments 43-44, 100

Making predictions/drawing conclusions 8-9, 15, 16, 22

Multiple-meaning words 185

Narrative elements 28-29, 46, 53

Sequence 59-60, 68, 76

Summarizing/paraphrasing 122-123, 130-131, 140

Summarizing the literature 4, 11, 18, 24, 32, 39, 48, 56, 62, 70, 78, 86, 95, 102, 111, 118, 125, 133, 142, 150, 157, 166, 173, 181

Synthesizing 137-138

LITERARY APPRECIATION

Dialogue 21, 30

Figurative language 82-83, 186

Imagery 176-177

Mood/tone 114

Point of view 170

DECODING

Structural analysis 36-37, 45, 54

SPELLING

Changing *y* to *i* 113

Compound words 88

Homophones 144

Irregular plurals 135

Prefixes *dis-, un-, mis-,* and *pre-* 104

Suffixes *-less, -ful, -ment,* and *-ness* 152

Words that end with *-ed* and *-ing* 72

VCV 175, 183

VCCV 159, 168

Words that end with /əl/ and /ən/ 127

Words that end with /ər/ 120

Words that end with *-y* and *-ey* 97

Words with /är/, /ôr/, and /âr/ 50

Words with *ie, ei,* and *eigh* 80

Words with long and short *a* 6

Words with long and short *e* 13

Words with long and short *i* 26

Words with long and short *o* and *u* 20

Words with /oo/ and /o͞o/ 41

Words with /ou/ and /oi/ 64

Words with /s/ and /j/ 34

Words with /yo͞or/ and /ûr/ 58

SKILLS AND STRATEGIES INDEX

STUDY SKILLS
Graphic aids 51–52
Reference sources 128–129, 139, 148

GRAMMAR
Adjectives and articles 87
Adjectives that compare 96
Adverbs 167
Adverbs that compare 174
Common and proper nouns 49
Complete, simple, and compound
   predicates 40
Complete, simple, and compound subjects
   33
Future tense 158
Negatives 182
Nouns, singular and plural 57
   possessive, singular and plural 63

Present tense and past tense 143
Pronouns
   possessive 79
   subject/object 71
Sentences
   Declarative/interrogative 5
   Exclamatory/imperative 12
   Simple/compound 19
Subjects and predicates 25
Verbs
   Action verbs 103
   Helping verbs 126
   Irregular verbs 151
   Linking verbs 112
   Main verbs 119
   Verb tenses 134